The Colour of My Underwear is... BLUE!

The
Colour
of My
Underwear
is...

BLUE!

TAG Publishing, LLC
2618 S. Lipscomb
Amarillo, TX 79109
www.TAGPublishers.com

Office (806) 373-0114
Fax (806) 373-4004
info@TAGPublishers.com

ISBN: 978-1-59930-174-7

Cover & Text: Lloyd Arbour, www.tablloyd.com

First Edition

DEDICATION:

To Don and Ruth Lyon.
Two ultra-fantastic people and incredible parents.

TESTIMONIALS

"This book is a simple-to-use guide to create the life of your dreams. It's brilliant the way Danny's carefully interwoven exercises throughout the book. Writing causes thinking ... thinking creates an image ... the image stirs emotions ... emotions cause action ... action sets up a reaction ... which sets up a new and improved result ... all of which is the essence of the Law of Attraction."

— Bob Proctor, As featured in The Secret
and best-selling author of You Were Born Rich, www.bobproctor.com

"I can't say enough about Lyon's ability to describe the necessities of moving forward while providing excellent tools to get there. Buy this book, read it, and lead yourself to what you want."

— Frank Kickbush, Author of
"The Secrets of Self-Leadership", www.frankkickbush.com

"Clear, concise and upbeat, Danny Lyon can relate to everyone through his experiences. He is able to guide you down the path to both a successful life and a successful business, one step at a time. The only thing stopping you from being successful is you.

—W.R. (Bill) Batdorf, Fiber Optic Specialist, ALTA Telecom Inc.

"This book will completely change how you look at your successes, how you plan for future growth and success, and will impress you on how easy it is to map out and take action."

—Doug Meharg, Author of "Become a Richer You", www.kidsridetoriches.com

"The Colour of my Underwear is Blue" is compelling reading. Delightfully entertaining with personally revealing stories packed full of powerful success principles and exercises."

—Andrew Barber-Starkey, Master Certified Coach, **The ProCoach Success System**, www.ProCoachSystem.com

"Easy to understand, easy to implement, Lyon's experiences and insights make this book a great investment in personal and business success."

—Dan Rodriguez, Entrepreneur, Author of "Anything with Two Heads is a Freak"

"Way above and beyond what I expected, this book delivers exactly what it says it will as Danny Lyon energizes and inspires all to overcome any obstacles."

—Shawn Shewchuk, Author and Consultant, www.changeyourresults.com

"Lyon's ongoing mission to help others succeed is evident as he provides effective tools that leave no doubt about everyone's ability to plan, grow and attain everything they want. "

—Anita Selby, Recreation Therapist, Author of "Re-Create the Seniors' Soul"

"Danny Lyon has a down-to-earth, humorous and direct style of sharing key concepts critical for success – your success!! His stories are funny and interesting and yet they also include a powerful message that can help you achieve your dreams and goals. Do yourself a huge favour and add this book to your library of success books. You'll be glad you did!!"

—Sonja Skage, Real Estate Investor

"I am privileged to recommend Danny Lyon's unstoppable best seller **The Colour Of My Underwear is Blue***. This amazing author lives his creed in relationships, business and service. Let this book's honesty and humility inspire and enlighten you. Your loved ones and team members will thank you as you apply its' practical yet life-changing information."*

—Barbara Arnold-Herzer R.N., L.M.T., Coach,
Speaker, Facilitator, Author

"I started to read this book casually and after the first couple of sentences I **wanted** *to read more. An enjoyable easy read that is informative and very educational. I am fortunate to have had the honour. This book's inspiration is just the prescription the Doctor ordered."*

—Cynthia Carpenter, Author,
Entrepreneur and Personal Trainer

The Colour of My Underwear is Blue is a fun, real life book dealing with what it takes to be truly successful. You will want this book to be part of your library for continual reference.

—Tammy Johnston: Founder & President of the Financial Guides,
www.thefinancialguides.com

CONTENTS

ACKNOWLEDGMENTS:

I am grateful for the support of so many people who helped create all of my successes and helped make this book possible. Thank-you to:

- Everyone from Barons, Alberta, Paradise - a fantastic place to grow up in.

- Robbie Cowie, a great friend to this day.

- Roy and Dorothy Dayman for their many lessons in life and business;

- Don (Kat) Keturakis, Billy Batdorf, & Ron Hillmer, the Technicians from Hell, for being so influential to a small town boy as a Telecom Technician on the road.

- Every teammate and coach in any sport I have played. There is no bigger privilege than being on a team, supporting others and allowing them to support you.

- All of my mentors in business that I have been fortunate enough to cross paths with.

- All of The UPS Store/Mail Boxes Etc. Franchisees from our Area, past and present.

- Ralph and Lisa Askar, mentors, motivators, business partners and good friends.

- The "ProCoach" – the amazing Master Certified Coach Andrew Barber-Starkey.

- My Inner Circle Mastermind for providing relentless inspiration and kicks in the butt.

- Hall of Fame Coach George Gemer who motivated & trained me for my first marathon.

- Runners Soul and the Runners Soul Marathon Club, www.runnersoul.com

- Cynthia Kersey, bestselling author and founder of Unstoppable Enterprises Inc. (www.unstoppable.net), for providing me the opportunity to help build schools in Kenya.

- My Grandparents, Alvan and Anna Lyon, for taking me everywhere and supporting every dream I had. Hardly a day goes by without a Nana Banana or Bumpa story.

- Numerous uncles, aunts, cousins, nephews, nieces and "in-laws" especially: my cousin Terry Lyon, a great athlete, who taught me how to throw a baseball and how to curl; my cousin Wade Lyon who is a pillar of support to everyone he comes in contact with; my Auntie Mae for her relentless encouragement and support to everyone in the family; and my Uncle Roy who taught me the importance of being able to sell.

- Business partner Kathy Campbell for building a successful business while raising two great daughters, Breanne and Katie, by herself.

- My brother Bobby for knowing early in life what he wanted and staying the course in his drive to achieve it.

- My sister Penny for being the worrier for us all, and always promoting the strength of family.

- My brother Jimmy for creating the challenges a free spirit seems to naturally create and incessantly believing and promoting, to this very day, that the best is yet to come.

- To Little Donny and Big Ruthie, Mom and Dad, for providing discipline, pushing that we think BIG, allowing and supporting growth and knowledge, and for showing me the ins and outs of work ethic and running a business.

- Of course, Tommy, Davey and Maggie Lyon, the greatest, most ultra-fantastic beings on earth, for making me the most successful person in the world even just by their existence, and for never doubting (at least publicly in my presence) that anything their dad tries could end in anything but success.

- And to The Beautiful and Vivacious Mrs. Connie Lyon for first finding me, then sticking with me and keeping everything together – as well as supporting all dreams and projects, including supporting every word of this book.

FOREWORD

I've been in business most of my life. I have spent the past 30 years helping others get into their own business while passionately teaching, mentoring, supporting and motivating them to attain success. I am frequently asked to share my business and success experiences and insights. It was a distinct honor when Danny asked me to write the foreword for *The Colour of My Underwear is Blue*.

I've known Danny Lyon for almost fourteen years now and have "been there" for many of his business successes. More importantly, I have observed his development, both on a personal and professional level, seeing how he leads by example. He is a master action taker.

The information presented in *The Colour of My Underwear is Blue* will help you realize that success is a choice - your choice. It will encourage you to look in the mirror to face tough questions. Why don't I do what I know I should be doing to reach my goals? Why am I so afraid to take more risks when risks typically bring out the best in me? Why don't I live with more passion and purpose and energy and fun? Why don't I attain more success towards my goals, dreams and desires?

After you read this book you will be armed with tools to turn questions into actions as you accelerate on the road to success with a network, a support team, that has always been there for you whether you realized it or not. This book provides steps for you and your network to create a better world for you – which creates a better world for everyone around you.

This book is really a workbook. It is a great read but don't just read it. Make sure you follow through and complete the exercises. If you do, you will never again be stuck in a rut or have lacklustre results. You will discover just how much support there is for you and that you are full of passion and energy – a person with purpose and full of action. You will discover that exponential success was always your choice and always within you.

— Ralph Askar
President and CEO, Instant Imprints
www.instantimprints.com

INTRODUCTION

How many of you would like more success?

How many of you would like more success faster?

Well, you have come to the right place. My name is Danny Lyon and…

THE COLOUR OF MY UNDERWEAR IS BLUE!

Coming from a business owning family in a small town, and after over 20 years of working in telecommunications, I have spent the last 14 years of my life running my own business, which includes helping other people get into business for themselves. It has been an amazing learning experience to see people from so many walks of life create such diverse levels of business success.

Some are *flying* full speed ahead right from the get-go. Some don't seem to be the right fit after they open and then suddenly turn things around, becoming hugely successful. Some build their business to a certain level and resist the extra effort to grow it any further. Some, who have all of the tools and should be flying full speed ahead, don't ever get out of the hangar or off the tarmac. Others fail just by giving up.

The exact same parallels exist in people's personal success as well. We all know people who are flying full speed ahead and others who have all of the talent in the world but don't seem to ever get it together. There are those that resist progress, growth and new experiences past certain comfort levels and we all know others that just give up.

I have found the same in sports. Many of the most talented athletes are not necessarily the most successful. There are also people out there, who have every reason to *give up*, but don't, and make the team or are out running marathons and inspiring those around them.

The most successful people are the ones that are the most open and honest with the situations they are in. They receive support because of their openness, and then take action with renewed confidence. My discovery was that the more people *expose* themselves (i.e. reveal *The Colour of Their Underwear*, figuratively speaking of course), the more they create opportunities for others to help them in their quest for personal, career or business success.

This holds true for the flip side as well. Individuals unwilling to open up or *expose* more about themselves or their situations, tend not to receive as much help from others. This type of person appears to build an imaginary fence, as if safe in their self-imposed, and many times self-destructive, enclosure. This does not have to be. No matter how bad things seem, or how unattainable goals appear to be, all that is needed is to *expose The Colour of Their Underwear*, and help will come.

When you let people know what you need, you are moving in the right direction with the right intent. Other people want to help you. They want to relate their life experiences and give you their knowledge. They want to help because…they just do.

If one takes the time to look closely, the list of people who influence and contribute to a person's successes is long. The kids you grew up with; the teachers, doctors, dentists, chiropractors; your coaches, parents, siblings, relatives, in-laws, co-workers, friends, customers, business partners, mentors, and many others. All of these people have been influential in some way. Some of the support you recognize without much thought. Some you may acknowledge regularly. Some you give credit to because they pushed you to excel or succeed. Some because they showed, or they taught, or they advised at the right time. Some because they tried to stop you or told you that you couldn't do something, so you proved them wrong. Others may not want you to succeed for whatever reason and they "help" you by providing hard lessons in who to trust, who to associate with and who to seek advice from.

You have already attracted many of the "right" people. My belief is that if you had exposed yourself more to these people, to the world, and to yourself, they and others could have helped you much more. This act no longer needs to be in the past tense.

My desire is that you will take a closer look at your successes plus the people who have contributed. That you will take action to grow yourself even further by revealing your new found knowledge about yourself and where you want to go. My desire is that you will "Expose Yourself for Success" to all of those around you and let them help you attain every dream and desire. They do indeed want to help you. They just need to know *The Colour of Your Underwear*.

At the same time that this is occurring, you will naturally be contributing back. Just like so many people have contributed to your successes, you influence and contribute to other people's successes. What makes their story so amazing is that *YOU* are in it. Think about that for a moment. That is a huge success for you, so start your own success list off with "**One of my successes is that I contribute to other people's success.**" The more you help others, the more help you will attract on your quest for a happy, successful life.

Give somebody a high five and say "Bring it on"!

Turn the pages and let's get on with the "exposure".

To Your Success,

Danny Lyon

CHAPTER 1:

– Networking Ooh La La! –

"The nice part about living in a small town is that when you don't know what you're doing, someone else does"

— Unknown

How frustrating it would be to go it alone!

PARADISE

It was about 2:30 pm on a weekday when the phone rang. My little brother, Jimmy, and I were having our afternoon nap in our bedroom. I was about 4-years-old and Jimmy was a year and some younger.

It was Mrs. MacQuarrie. She asked, "Ruth, isn't Jimmy supposed to be having his nap right now?" My Mother answered "Yes". "Well, he just rode past my house on his tricycle", said Mrs. MacQuarrie. My Mother came into our room, woke me up, and together we discovered that my bedroom window was open and Jimmy had "escaped". Luckily, our house was a single story bungalow. Still, it was quite a jump for an adventurous, and apparently not tired, almost 3-year-old.

Only in a small town could getting caught this easily happen. Only in a small town would someone on the other side of town know who you were, which mother you belonged to, and also know your schedule.

Afternoon naps were nearly impossible to get out of and before getting turned in by the town's "secret police" so to speak (the "secret police" seemed to be everywhere), my brother's escape had been a great success. If he was doing the success exercise we are going to do later on, he could list "I once successfully escaped from my afternoon nap".

Every personal development course or seminar I have ever been to suggests that to accomplish anything you need to:

1. Know what you want;

2. Prioritize activities; and then

3. Take action.

Jimmy slept in the top bunk and could stare at the ceiling when formulating good ideas. As a bottom bunk dweller "and I know there are others of you out there" when I laid on my back I stared at the springs of my brother's bed. I spent more time wondering what damage my body might incur if the wooden cross beams holding up his bed ever snapped, as opposed to formulating gutsy ideas like escaping from an afternoon nap. Imagine my brother staring at the ceiling, determining he was not sleepy that afternoon, and then devising a plan to do something else. At only almost 3-years-old, Jimmy followed the success formula to the letter.

1. He knew what he wanted.
   He wanted to do something other than sleep – like ride his tricycle around town.

2. He prioritized and planned his actions.
   Get out of the room, get out of the house, and get out of the yard.

3. Then Jimmy took action. The "Do It" part.
   He got down from the top bunk, got his pants and shoes on,

got the window open, crawled out, hung off the window ledge and dropped to the ground – all without waking me up. He located his tricycle and wheeled out of our yard without our mother spotting him from one of the windows of our house.

Jimmy was successful. And I was jealous. He did what so many only dreamed about – escape from their afternoon nap. If the "secret police" had not gotten involved, Jimmy may have made it back to our house later and no one would have known any different.

Barons, Alberta Canada is a town of about 250 people, and it was the centre of the universe, or so it seemed. Rarely a day in my life goes by where Barons isn't mentioned or comes up in a conversation from someone else. Perhaps that is how it is for everyone and the community where they grew up.

The small town model is a good one for analyzing how strong a network of support can be. Even if you grew up in or live in a large city, there are small town aspects in each area of that city and in most places of employ.

I truly believe growing up in my self-proclaimed small town "paradise" and learning the people skills and service skills that come with everyone knowing everyone (plus the name of their dog and cat), is what has helped me in all successes in my life, both personal and in business.

The Village of Barons had a bustling main street, a school from grades one to nine, and an agricultural based rural population to draw from. The really important things to a kid were a lake several miles out of town, the best vacation spot in the world – the Rocky Mountains – a short drive straight west, a skating rink, a curling rink, a baseball diamond, railway tracks on the west side of town, a number of empty lots where any kind of game could be played, and just enough abandoned buildings to explore and to get us into trouble from time to time.

Looking back, the main activity of the town was networking. Perhaps it was the ultimate network model.

All networking environments satisfy the human need for community and socializing. At the same time an excellent support mechanism – as intrusive as it may be at times – becomes incredibly strong. Small communities like Barons accomplish outstanding things because of the willingness to protect and strengthen the community by working together, as a team.

The same networking environment principles apply to successful businesses, successful careers and personal successes – no matter where you grew up.

The team is stronger than the individual. I can say confidently that every successful person I have ever known had a strong team of support built from a strong network.

Small town athletics is a good example. Pick any sport – hockey, baseball, basketball, football, volleyball, etc. In many instances, it is amazing that small towns can produce enough players to field a team, let alone produce winning teams. A friend of mine always said that if you were old enough to tie your shoes, you were old enough to be on the team.

The strength of these teams comes from being together for so many years (networking) and no one ever saying that they couldn't or shouldn't win every game (motivation, support and confidence from the network). The ability to work as a team toward a common vision is what Andrew Carnegie said "is the fuel that allows common people to attain uncommon results".

We live in the city now and, a few years ago, my son Tommy's team won the Grade Nine District Volleyball Championships against a team from a small town. The final went to three sets and either team could have won. On the way home, Tommy would not believe that the small town team could be "that good", considering that the population of his school was about double the population of the *whole town* the other team came from. Teamwork, trust and support for the common vision leads to uncommon results and, in this case, almost a District Championship.

I believe being on a team and being a *team player* is the key to success – in sports or otherwise. Pick any successful person you can think of and you'll see they will not have achieved their level of success without help. Whether it be help from their team mates, coaches, associates, employees, advisors, customers, vendors, family, or friends, etc.; no one did it on their own. They needed the support of their network. You too need the support of your network.

EXPOSE YOURSELF

It is much more difficult for your network to help you and support your wants, needs, goals and desires if you are not open and willing to "expose" yourself to them.

In a small town environment it was easy, sometimes too easy, to be exposed. The place we were most exposed was at school.

"Education is learning what you didn't
even know you didn't know".

— Daniel J. Boorstin

School is one of the first instances of organized networking that a person experiences. School also comes with commitment, discipline and set structure. In my opinion, the social aspect, the networking, is the most important benefit of school.

It was about a 15 minute walk, diagonally corner to corner, across Barons and 5 minutes or less on a bike. We "town" kids had to enter Barons Consolidated High School from the front doors in the morning (girls in the east doors and boys in the west doors) and we had to go home for lunch during the school day unless we had written permission to stay for lunch because our parents were away. At the end of the school day we had to again exit from the front doors – girls east, boys west. God forbid if we town kids ever got caught entering the school in the morning or exiting at the final bell from the back doors where the "out-of-town" kids loaded onto the busses. I am not sure what the punishment would have been but it was just something we avoided. Recesses and lunch breaks on the playground were filled mostly with double-scrub softball, the search for mice in the Caragana trees, mastery of the monkey bars, football and honouring the playground pecking order. Football was usually town kids against the out-of-town kids and it was a historic day in our Barons Consolidated School life when my cousin Wadey Lyon and his family moved into town in Grade 6. Wadey became a town kid that day. Wadey was stronger than all of us and extremely difficult to tackle. He became our "in-town" team mate and the "out-of-town" team's problem.

In the winter, if it was too cold to go outside during the breaks, we played in the gym. My recollection is that there were very few times we were ever in the gym. I remember bundling up and heading outdoors most of the time in the winter. Of course, as my kids have heard many times now, those were the days of 40 foot snow drifts, freezing winds and we still had to walk to school (uphill both ways of course).

A small school in a small town meant small classes and the fact that teachers could spend more time with you. We didn't know it at the time but we were privileged to have an education in that environment. There were 8 of us in our grade nine graduating class, making it pretty hard to slip under the radar – academically or for behaviour. Basically, someone was always close by to hold us accountable – and accountability is extremely important for results and success in school, in business, in careers, and in life.

In my family, getting in trouble at school meant you were in even bigger trouble at home. Disrespecting school property or a teacher was not tolerated. So it was possible to get the "strap" at school and a 'licken' (parent slang for a spanking) at home on the same day for the same thing. Good incentive to "mind your P's and Q's" or my dad's favourite line, "govern yourself accordingly".

There was no way to cover up the fact you had gotten into trouble at school either. Everyone in town knew in short order. Besides classmates telling all, the teachers were only teachers by day. They were also active members of the community, perhaps more accessible and visible than teachers in larger centres.

I remember getting the strap in Grade 5 from Miss. Sonmor, and thought I could slide it under the rug with my parents. My hope was that, if it ever came up, it would be far enough into the future that the threat of punishment would be lessened. I arrived home for supper, bounced up the stairs from our back porch and stopped in my tracks as there was Miss. Sonmor sitting at our kitchen table. My mom had invited her for supper. No place for me to hide. Exposed again.

Who we were going through school, who we hung out with, who we allowed to help us, and who we pushed away were so important in early successes and failures and set the stage for future successes. The good part is that, although school eventually ends, education does not. The importance of networking and having as large a network as possible is as important for confidence, knowledge, and accomplishment now, no matter where we are in our lives, as it was when we were kids.

Success and one's network go hand in hand. Exposing oneself for success takes a certain level of sincerity and vulnerability. It is about giving opinions, sharing dreams, sharing beliefs and sharing goals.

 DANNY DIAMOND SUCCESS TIP:

Since everyday is an acting job in which you get to choose how you act or what role you play, choose to be upbeat and choose to enjoy the day.

You get to choose your attitude every step of the way.

First and foremost, be a team player.

The key to utilizing your network for success is to be sincere about who you are and what you are about. Be willing to "drop the act". You will soon realize that any self-proclaimed flaws are not flaws at all to those in your network – at least not to the ones who want the best for you. Exposing yourself to as many people as possible will   remove a huge weight from your shoulders. It will be great knowledge for you and will provide the opportunity for your network to help you grow in leaps and bounds.

COMMUNICATION

In the framework of Networking Ooh La La!, communication relates to the importance of keeping as many people as possible updated and informed on a regular basis. In business it can be with partners, business associates, staff, and suppliers on one hand and customers (through the many avenues of marketing) on the other. In your personal life it can be with family or significant others on one hand and friends and mentors on the other.

A critical aspect of *exposing yourself for success* is that good communication leads to better problem solving, enhanced creativity and assists with converting plans into action. I am betting you already have a large number of people waiting to support you whole-heartedly with the taking action part of a plan. Communicating openly, honestly and regularly, you will build better personal and working relationships within your network and they will carry you on their shoulders by increasing your confidence and opening up opportunities for you.

CONSISTENCY

People bounce around from one idea to the next, even one job or business venture to the next. In the world today, the fast pace lends itself to a lack of direction and many times lack of loyalty – loyalty to people, careers, education.

Consistency, your consistency, is a key to great networking and is one of the foundations in the small town model discussed earlier. This consistency is another key factor in the *exposing of oneself for success*. Those in your network need to know that the person they are networking with, **you**, will show up, will not take your eye off the ball, and will take the action necessary to move forward – as most everyone says they want to do.

In the same respect, your network needs to be able to depend on your consistent support, your contribution to their needs and goals, as well as the discipline to hold them accountable if they get off track.

INTEGRITY

Honesty and trust are the backbone of anyone's network and to obtain results, being face to face with your peers in complete integrity is perhaps the most important part of the exposure.

You can be daring in your growth and desires and perhaps sometimes impractical. When you're coming from integrity each and every time, you will receive whole-hearted support from your network. You need to *expose* your sincerity and honesty each time so that the trust level is high enough for them to act with integrity in supporting you. Many of you reading this are already leaders and many, many more of you will become leaders. Integrity is the foundation of good leadership.

Buckminster Fuller said it best when he said, "Integrity is the essence of everything successful."

ASK

It's been said that when you ask someone a question you are empowering them.

Some questions revolve around looking for a solution to a problem, fulfilling a need or want, or the completion of a simple action. But with each question, regardless of the type, you are empowering the other person, giving them the opportunity if you will, to solve the puzzle.

The same is true when you ask yourself a question. How much more could you answer on the subject of your dreams and goals on a journey to success? What if you empowered yourself with a steady flow of questions and had a bunch that you didn't know the answer to? That is where your network comes in. Ask them. Empower them. And they will help.

If you don't ask, the answer is always "no". Therefore, asking about the possibilities on any subject, goal or idea opens up the opportunity for a "yes". Yes I can do this. Yes I believe I could attain this.

So ask, and ask often about everything. Ask yourself as well as those around you.

TEAMWORK

Having team mates started when you were born. The doctor and nurses in the delivery room automatically became part of YOUR team. Then your family, friends, teachers, coaches, bosses, co-workers, customers, etc., everyone you come in contact with, good or bad, all naturally join your team as you go through life.

Bob Proctor states, "The main thing is to keep the main thing the main thing." That main thing refers to your growth, your success and you attaining your dreams and desires. If you are able to keep your main thing focus, you will attract solid team mates. Good team mates and great teamwork promotes exponential growth and creates more confidence and faster movement forward. The team also keeps you accountable to yourself and to every other team member.

Teamwork and the power of many sharing one purpose = amazing results.

SPORTS

Most of us can relate to sports because we either played a sport or two growing up and/or we watch sports live in our area or on TV.

There are three special aspects of sports that relate to good team work, which relates to good networking, which relates to your success.

Rules: Sports have rules that a team or individual must work within. Rules set the guidelines of focus for any team.

Motivation: Motivation comes from the coach, of course, the players, the parents and the fans. Motivation comes from wanting to do well on behalf of the team and from seeing team mates do well. Motivation comes from the fact that others will go out of their way to help you if it is for the betterment of the team.

Coaching - the best part. Every successful person has a coach – whether in sports or in life. The coach directs, instructs, and trains to achieve way beyond what one could have done on your own.

Your network, *your* team, will have all three, formed through the communication and integrity of those you associate with.

Motivation goes without saying. If your network does not get you jazzed, get you motivated and you don't do the same for them, then it is time to make some changes.

Your network is a natural coach. As you ask openly and honestly for what you need, your network will direct, instruct, train and support. You can also add life coaches, business coaches, physical trainers, nutritionalists, etc. to your network. All designed to help you grow and hold you accountable.

COMPETITION

Keeping in the same vein of team work and sports for a moment longer, the main ingredient of both is competition. Competition increases drive and desire within oneself and this also entails adaptation. This means adapting to the roadblocks or obstacles that get in our way. How we adapt and how we handle situations is much easier with the backing of a solid team, a solid network, who can coach us and guide us.

So, welcome competition. At first, at whatever level you are comfortable with. Then expand outside your comfort zone to challenge yourself, adapting as you go. Those within your network will help, just as you can help them. I believe the experience of added competition will make what seemed to be a major roadblock shrink or go away.

NETWORKING BY DEFAULT

Every day in every way.

You are consistently adding to and taking away from your network daily. Just by living, by working, by getting up in the morning, we come in contact with many people and many opportunities. Everyone may not make *your* "team". However, whether you are at lunch, at a networking meeting, at school, at work, at the front counter in your business or at your kid's sporting event, you are constantly around other people who have great life experience. Perhaps they have great experience in some of what you want out of life.

So be on your toes and ensure you "network by default" as opportunities can come from anywhere.

ENTREPRENEURSHIP

Everywhere in this book that I mention the word "business", it can also relate to "job" or "career" or "profession". Most importantly, it also refers to "personal" because in my experience business and personal are synonymous.

When one's business, job, career, or profession is humming along, doing well, a quick look at one's personal life will typically mirror business results. Because really, even if those in your personal life – spouses or partners, kids, family, friends - don't seem directly involved in your business, make no mistake, they are indeed involved and in a big way. Their understanding and support of what it takes to make your business successful, or to 'bring home the bread', is crucial.

 ### DANNY DIAMOND SUCCESS TIP:

Involve your family and friends in as many of your business, job, career or profession get-togethers, projects, and special events as possible. Be willing to share as much information as possible with them - *Expose yourself.*

DANNY DIAMOND SUCCESS TIP:

As a supporter of a family member or friend that has a business, job, career or profession, you should be open to listening, being proactive in supporting them, and taking advantage of the opportunities to join them at get-togethers, projects or special events. Why? Because what you give you get. By gaining a better understanding of what it takes for the other person to 'bring home the bread', it greatly improves the most important "personal" side of things.

Really, we are all running home based businesses – whether it has that official title or not. We just have different names for it like home, family, bills, cars and jobs, instead of store front, staff, inventory, expenses and customers.

When the word entrepreneur is mentioned, most of us think of a business person, large projects and lots of money. But we are all entrepreneurs. An entrepreneur is really someone who starts an enterprise, who utilizes a network of contacts and associates to help them get the work done, and who is constantly looking for money to put towards the project's completion and seeing it become successful. Doesn't that describe all of us in our personal lives as well?

Didn't we all start an enterprise as soon as we were born and don't we keep starting projects as we grow through life? Don't we constantly utilize the help of others? Aren't we constantly looking for money as we work towards the successful completion of our projects? I hereby dub you an entrepreneur, if you didn't already think you were one. Tell your family, friends, associates, customers, etc. that you are an entrepreneur – tell everyone.

In relation to networking and success, it is the qualities of an entrepreneur we want to look at, not just the name or title.

An entrepreneur is about planning, about opportunity, about drive and determination. All great qualities if one wants to get on the road to success in an accelerated fashion. And the entrepreneur has to have respect for others, act in integrity, and be consistent or he or she will not be an entrepreneur very long - at least not one that gets to see the projects become successful.

SMALL TOWN MODEL

I believe we all have the potential to work from a small town networking model, where maximum support can be obtained. This does not mean small numbers because it is a small town model. Your network should be as large as possible and ever growing. The small town networking model I am referring to is one of maximum exposure with focused vision that leads to uncommon results. Let's tie it all together and do an exercise to build your list of network participants and perhaps the realization of network members who are already chomping at the bit to help you.

As you work through the following exercises, look for and be open to breakthroughs in: **discoveries** of just how big networking can be; **opportunities** that you did not see before; **overcoming** the prejudging of anyone.

For Networking Ooh La, La! to be most effective, be confident in your abilities to "Ask", "Be direct", "Have No expectations (don't prejudge)", "Be reliable, "Be giving (willing to return a favour for someone else)", and "Remove the negative people".

In building your list below **Family** is the place to start. They generally have the same or similar beliefs as you do (whether that is good or bad you can decide later). They connected with you the most at some part of your life, if not now.

The second category for consideration in your list is **Friends**. Friends are typically supportive, provide feedback, and most respect you. I recommend listing friends that are close, friends that are not that close, and even former friends. List them all. Go as far back as you can remember.

Associates and acquaintances are the next category. These are people you have worked with, been on the same team with - in business, your career, school, sports, etc. Work through your history and open yourself to listing everyone.

A natural and very important extension of all categories is your **Mentors** list. Mentors are those that have provided you with expertise, confidence and development. They are the ones, in your mind, who are wise and trusted, who pulled or pull for you to win. Mentors are typically ones that have already done what you are trying to do. They help you in not having to re-invent the wheel. Please highlight them.

EXERCISE 1: *Make the list.*

Using all of the idea stimulators around family, friends, associates, acquaintances and mentors, complete the following exercise.

* Note: a template of this form is available at www. thecolourofmyunderwearisblue.com

BUILD A LIST OF OVER 100 PEOPLE AS A MINIMUM. (Don't stop at just 100)

MY NETWORKING OOH LA LA!

Name	Relation/ Category (family, friend, associate, acquaintances, mentor, etc.)	Most influencing aspect of this person	Time in my life of most influence (ex. now; 1995; last year; in school, childhood, etc.)

EXERCISE 2: *Identifying influence.*

1. Take out a fresh sheet of paper.

2. In the very center of the page draw a small circle and write "ME" in the middle of the circle.

3. Utilizing the network list you created in Exercise #1, draw small circles on the page to represent those in the list. Put their name or initials inside the circle drawn so that you can remember who they are.

***VERY IMPORTANT: draw each circle in such a way as to correspond how close you feel the person is to you as of the current date. In other words, if the person is really close to you or influential in real life, put their circle closer to your "ME" circle on the page. If a person is not that close to you (in your opinion, not theirs), then draw their circle further away from your "ME" circle on the page.

You will ultimately end up with all or most of your network list represented on the page with circles. They will be various distances from your "ME" circle in relation to how close you feel they are to you.

* Note: a template of this form is available at www.thecolourofmyunderwearisblue.com

4. Now, look at each circle and focus on that person for a moment. Be really honest with yourself as to whether that person is helping or hindering you on the road to success (be it personal, business or career success).

What you are doing in step 4 is making a judgment on whether or not it would be better for you to move closer to a particular person, or move away from that person.

Be very honest. Go through each one and assess whether they are helping you become who you want to be and as successful as you want to be. Or, are they holding you back or perhaps are a negative influence in other ways.

Then, draw an arrow pointing away from your "ME" circle beside the circles of any person you want to move away from, or distance yourself from.

Then draw an arrow pointing towards your "ME" circle beside the circles of any person you should or want to move towards and become closer to.

A very enlightening exercise, I believe you will be surprised at some of the results.

An example of what your sheet may look like follows.

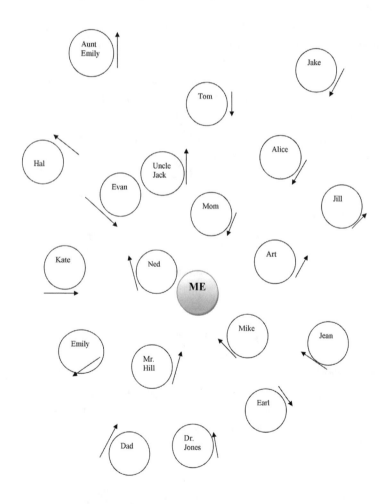

EXERCISE 3: *Prioritize the list.*

Using the information from identifying your influence circles in Exercise 2, re-do your Networking Ooh La La! list in priority sequence. Move the people who are the most influential and you want to be the closest to higher up on the list. Move those that you indicated you want or need to move away from further down the list.

SUMMARY

Life in a small town, to me, was an exercise in "Exposing Yourself for Success" everyday. It was about being upfront and open to people, whether the information was offered freely (the preferred method) or they found out through the grapevine and you had to come clean. I learned that so many people could help others. I learned that so many people *want* to help others. They can make you accountable, so that you become more accountable to yourself.

Now that you have completed the exercises you have a list of your network as you know it today – and you have perhaps learned something about who you thought you were close to and who might have been holding you back.

 DANNY DIAMOND SUCCESS TIP:

Never stop growing your list. It should become a living, ever expanding document as you continue to add people into your network. "*Expose yourself*" – open up with your plans, needs and desires.

Remember, that with each person you add to your network, you create additional opportunities for success in every realm you desire. And, just as important, you create the same opportunities to help each person attain their successes.

CHAPTER 2:

— I Made You Say Underwear —

He behaved like an ostrich and put his head in the sand, thereby exposing his thinking parts.

— George Carman

Take a look at the picture of me on www.thcolourofmyunderwearis-blue.com. Now imagine that guy, a whole bunch younger, dressed up (or really dressed down) for Halloween as a baby, completely naked except for a white bed sheet made into a diaper (note that I had a pair of underwear, probably blue, on underneath).

My date and I were at the Annual Halloween Dance in Barons, Alberta, Canada; paradise – the Centre of the Universe. Even though it was the end of October and cold, for whatever reason, I had not brought along a shirt, a coat, a pair of socks....nothing. The only things I had were my "diaper", the all important underwear underneath, and a pair of old running shoes that had long ago been abandoned in the back of my car.

In those *olden days* my drink of favour was Vodka and Coke. If over consumption ever took place, I contracted a lazy eye problem where my left eye would involuntarily close for the evening. This pretty much gave away the state I was in well in advance of trying to communicate with me.

At sometime on this particular evening, I did something wrong that upset my date. I don't know what it was, and will probably never know, but I would bet that my left eye being closed had something to do with it. Whatever I did, it was bad enough that we were leaving and I was to drive her home…NOW!

I should not have been driving of course but this was a long time ago when more people tended to do stupid things in that regard. The next problem was it was not just a simple drive to a house in Barons. Instead, it was a drive to Lethbridge, 30 miles away, in my 1975 Honda Civic with a two speed heater fan. A two speed fan in the Prairie winter, on the highway, meant you ended up with a single defrosted spot on the windshield just above the dash of only about 6 inches in diameter.

So, after not letting the car warm up for as long as normal because getting her home NOW was the priority, we headed out. There I was, hunched over, trying to see out that small clear spot on my windshield with my left eye closed. I was shivering and my teeth were chattering from insufficient heating and nothing on but a bed sheet made into a diaper. My date provided a loud lecture on whatever it was I had done wrong for the whole trip to Lethbridge. I had decided that using the back roads was a better idea than risking running into a police officer, or anyone else, on the main highway. It seemed like hours before I got her home. She didn't even give me a kiss good night.

Now for the trip back home.

I made my way down 6th Avenue South in Lethbridge and came to a red light right in front of the Lethbridge Curling Club. It was the middle of the night now and not a car was in sight. As I waited for the red light to change, I fell asleep, which wasn't hard to do since my left eye was already locked shut. When I woke up from my nap (which I remember hoping had only been for a few minutes), I made an executive decision that I should catch 20 winks - in a more appropriate place than at a traffic light - before tackling the drive home.

I backed up from the traffic light, which was still red but had probably changed from red to green to red several times while I was snoozing. I then angle parked right in front of the Lethbridge Curling Club front doors. Initially, I left the car running. When the heater finally caught up with the cold, as it would do when parked, I got too hot (even with only a diaper on). Instead of adjusting the heating controls, I simply shut the car off.

I woke up a few hours later to the sounds of my teeth chattering and the voices of people as they made their way into the Curling Club for their 8 am Saturday morning league games. Because I had chosen to park dead centre in front of the main doors of the club, everyone entering got to see the shivering, sleeping man dressed only in … a diaper? I quickly reached for the keys to start the car and get out of there. There was nothing but a click. I tried it again. NO! I had turned the engine off in the middle of the night but had left my lights on. The battery was dead. If I was cold before it suddenly felt much colder.

"Think man. How do you get out of this one?" I said to myself.

Note that the diaper was really a bed sheet made into a diaper. Not once during the whole night or morning did I think to take it off, unravel it and use it to keep warm or at least to cover myself up more.

As my mind raced to figure out a solution, the facts of the situation were these. I was a member of the Lethbridge Curling Club. I knew it was warm inside the club. I even had my curling pants and a sweater in my locker inside. Also, I knew a lot of people in the Curling Club. Probably more than one of the members would have had jumper cables to give my car a quick boost to get me on my way. Yet, I could not get past the perceived embarrassment I might suffer if I entered the rink dressed as I was. This I could not get over, even though most everyone in the club at the time had probably already seen me dressed as I was when they had walked past the car and into the club.

The solution was very clear in my groggy, "morning after" thoughts. I must call my cousin Wadey in Barons, Alberta, Canada; paradise – the Centre of the Universe - and he would save the day. Wadey could be counted on to always save the day. This was way before cell phones had been invented. Since I refused to enter the Curling Club where they had pay phones, the only other pay phone in the vicinity was on the other side of the running track directly adjacent to the Curling Club. If I could only get over to that phone, without being noticed, I could call Wadey and he would blast into Lethbridge, give me a boost, and we would be back home in no time.

My plan was to look like a jogger, of which there were 3 or 4 already on the track. It was now November 1st, freezing cold and I was more than slightly hung-over. Shivering like crazy, I was going to try to pass myself off as a jogger with no shirt, no coat, no long pants, no socks and no shoes. I saw no other way and decided to give it a try.

But wait! I did have shoes. I had the old abandoned pair in the back of the car. I crawled back to get them and was pleasantly surprised that they fit. At least they fit well enough for what I needed them for because, how many barefooted joggers does one ever see, let alone in November? I had Shoes! Things were looking up.

I exited the car only to discover that if you try to sleep in a 1975 Honda Civic on a very cold night with the heater off, one's legs get all cramped up. Even just standing beside the car was challenging. As blood started to flow, I started to walk over to the track. I purposely tried not to look at the front windows of the Curling Club or at the traffic passing by on the street adjacent to the club. My theory was, if I didn't look, then certainly no one would be looking at me. As I got on the track and jogged a bit, a couple of the other runners came up behind me and I heard them abruptly stop the conversation they had going on when they finally realized what was ahead of them on the track. They ran in silence while they passed and got ahead of me. Then when their conversation resumed, it was more of a whispering "what the hell was that?" tone.

It seemed like forever but I made it to the phone booth. Yes...I know you were thinking it but I did remember to bring coins. I called Wadey.

He too was hung-over from the dance. He argued profusely that I was loony for not just getting a boost from someone in the area, instead of asking him to drive the 30 miles into Lethbridge. In the end, after much begging and whining on my part, he agreed to save me. I requested that he also bring a jacket for me.

Now I had to get back to my car. No problem! I felt I had done such a good job of passing myself off as a jogger before that I would simply do it again. The good news is that the two runners who passed me on the way over to the phone booth were no longer on the track. The bad news was that there were now even more people using the track for their morning exercise. They were spread out such that there was not a gap big enough for me to slide into where I wouldn't be noticed. Yes, I was still thinking that I could get this done without being noticed.

It took me a long time to get brave enough to make the trek back to my car. I remember trying to justify to myself that the phone booth was maybe a nick warmer than my car anyway, but I eventually sucked it up and did my best jogger impression again. This time I had enough blood flowing through my legs that I could prevent anyone from passing me.

It seemed like only minutes after getting back to the car when Wadey showed up and with a jacket for me. Because everyone else had parked in front of the Curling Club as I had, there was no way for Wadey to get his car close enough to boost my car. From the perspective of two hung-over individuals, we decided that Wadey had to pull into the driveway entrance at the side of the Club, and then drive along the sidewalk to my car. No problem. That wouldn't attract any attention. We were able to boost my car in minutes and my life was saved. I then got to drive back home, hunched over, looking through the small clear space on my completely frozen windshield with the heater on full blast.

The moral to this story is two-fold. Firstly, had I had the courage to utilize my network, I could have made my life much easier by solving the problem much quicker. I was too busy worrying about what those going into the Curling Club might think, even though I knew most of them, as opposed to coming clean on my situation and asking for their help. I believe that we all could make life much easier if we exposed our situations, concerns and problems better, and let our network help us.

Secondly, although the majority of the evening and the aniticipation and planning for the event was a success, the focus automatically defaults to what caused the evening to have problems. Problems, for most people, are what makes the story the story, as opposed to all of the successes. Unfortunately, this seems to be the case with most things in life, both personal and in business. There is too much focus on the negative and the problems. Isn't that why everything in the media is more about the concerns, the problems, the mayhem, than it is about all of the good things happening?

In my experience, people rarely give as much time to focus on their successes as they do on their problems.

 DANNY DIAMOND SUCCESS TIP:

The exercise of regularly acknowledging your successes is one of the best stress relievers and providers of energy that there is.

First and foremost, you are successful. Right now, today, you are successful. For some it might not feel like you are, but you are. It doesn't matter how much money you have in the bank, how your marriage or relationships are working out, how the kids are doing in school, how much hair is left on your head, how much you weigh, what kind of shape you are in physically, who you owe money to, or how your date on Halloween went. All of us get to live through experiences riding the highs and suffering through the lows. Take a closer look and be honest with yourself. *Expose* yourself to the great network you acknowledged and created in Chapter #1. Together you can look at the successes that have already occurred and discover that you are indeed successful today. Then together, work on more success.

We tend to focus on what we didn't do or don't do; or didn't accomplish or don't accomplish; or didn't have or don't have. We like to blame things and people for the "did *not's*" and "do *not's*". We complain and we justify the situation or perceived predicament by making excuses.

We rarely focus on all of the good things we have done or that have happened to us and the people who were influential in those successes.

Let's do a Success Review together right now.

I learned to review successes quarterly through the business coaching of Andrew Barber-Starkey, an amazing Master Certified Coach from ProCoach Success System. For years my partners and I have completed the same exercise with people we have helped get into business at our quarterly networking meetings. I highly recommend this Success Review for everyone.

EXERCISE 4: *Success Review*

Step 1: I recommend you utilize the Review Sheet below, which is provided courtesy of Andrew Barber-Starkey, Master Certified Coach from ProCoach International Inc.

Before carrying on to the next step, ensure you have a blank Review Sheet in front of you to work from.

* Note: A copy of this review is available at http://www.procoachsystem. com/UnderwearQuarterlyReview

QUARTERLY PROGRESS REVIEW
(courtesy of ProCoach International Inc.)

Reflect on the past quarter or year to date and list 10 accomplishments, successes, areas of progress or positive events that occurred for you. Include work, business, personal, family, etc.

IDEA STIMULATORS

• Business milestones and progress • Business relationships – new & old • Leadership success • Personal & Professional development • Financial – income, investments, etc.	• Risks taken/going out of comfort zone • Presentations and speeches • Personal relationships – new & old • Events attended • Obstacles overcome • Completion and letting go	• New opportunities • Health & fitness • Home & family • Trips & vacations • Recreation • Spiritual • Community

1. _____
   _____
   _____

2. _____
   _____
   _____

3. _____
   _____
   _____

4. _____
   _____
   _____

5. _____
   _____
   _____

6. _____
   _____
   _____

7. _____
   _____
   _____

8. _____
   _____
   _____

9. _____
   _____
   _____

10. _____
    _____
    _____

What was the best decision you made in the last quarter?

_____
_____
_____

Listing the first thing that comes to mind, what was the biggest highlight of the year to date?

_____
_____
_____

Who are the 3 people who had the biggest impact on your life this year to date?

_____
_____
_____

1. _____
   _____
   _____

2. _____
   _____
   _____

3. _____
   _____
   _____

What are the most important lessons or principles you have learned this year to date?

1. _____
   _____
   _____

2. _____
   _____
   _____

3. _____
   _____
   _____

In what ways have you grown and developed as a person in the last quarter?

IDEA STIMULATORS

• Skills and abilities learned • New attitudes or perspectives. Qualities developed. Areas where confidence has increased
• Supportive habits developed • Non-supportive habits eliminated

1. _____
   _____
   _____

2. _____
   _____
   _____

3. _____
   _____
   _____

What are your most significant goals/areas of focus for the rest of the year?

1. _____
   _____
   _____

2. _____
   _____
   _____

3. _____
   _____
   _____

STEP 2:

Utilizing the blank Quarterly Review sheet above, sit down for a few minutes of quiet, and focus on successes - no matter how small.

Personal successes, relationship successes, successes with or about your children, academic successes, sports successes, job or career successes, business successes and any others.

Write down every success from the last week or month or quarter or however far you want to go back. If you need more sheets, print off more or use the back of the Quarterly Review.

In addition, write down everyone who contributed or helped you along the way with each success.

Then complete the rest of the Quarterly Review – best decision, biggest highlights, most impactful people, lessons learned, how you have grown, and goals you are focused on.

DANNY DIAMOND SUCCESS TIP:

This is YOU talking to YOU and acknowledging your successes. Be very generous and complimentary to yourself. Write fast and what first comes to mind – don't analyze too much.

DANNY DIAMOND SUCCESS TIP:

If you can't think of any successes or are struggling to list more than a few, then that is how it is normally for you. Never giving yourself enough credit. Quit thinking and start writing. Go ahead, pat yourself on the back for your successes. Take action. Write them down.

STEP 3: *Share.*

I know I said it was you talking to you but for the most impact, sharing your successes with others is exciting and loaded with positive energy. It leads to a new habit of focusing on sharing success stories, instead of the problem stories I mentioned earlier. A focus on sharing success stories will attract a whole new group of success driven, success oriented people into your network.

Did you have at least one success you did not realize was a success until you did the exercise?

_____ Yes   _____ No

Did you discover you had more successes, more wins, than you had been giving yourself credit for?

_____ Yes   _____ No

Was the exercise a difficult one for you?

_____ Yes   _____ No

With a little focus and effort, could you do this exercise with yourself and for yourself quarterly?

_____ Yes   _____ No

EXERCISE 5:

The network we have or create and our ability to be open and honest (*exposed*) to that network, is the foundation for all personal and business success.

You identified some of your network in Chapter 1.

You have just completed an exercise, a success review that provides a great vehicle in exposing yourself to your network.

Your success foundation is now in place.

Capitalize on this opportunity.

Please answer the following questions:

1. Were people from my network listing in Chapter 1 responsible for some of the successes in the Quarterly Success Review above?

_____ Yes   _____ No

2. If "Yes", list 3 to 5 people who seem to be having the most influence on your successes at present;

_____   _____

_____   _____

_____

3. If "No", do you feel you are doing too much on your own without asking for support or help?

_____ Yes   _____ No

4. List 3 to 5 people in your existing network who, if you had the confidence to call on them more (*expose yourself* to more), could help you attain even more and greater success than you have been experiencing or that became evident in the Quarterly Review exercise? (Note that some or all could be the same people you listed in #2 above)

_____   _____

_____   _____

_____

"At times our own light goes out and is rekindled by a spark from another person. Each of us has cause to think with deep gratitude of those who have lighted the flame within us. "

— Albert Schweitzer

**Review, Review, Review regularly.
Then re-plan and refocus.**

Celebrate all successes no matter how small.

Congratulations to you on all of your successes!

CHAPTER 3:

— *The Old Ball & Chain*—

"Twenty years from now you will be more disappointed by the things you didn't do than by the ones you did do. So throw off the bowlines. Sail away from the safe harbour. Catch the trade winds in your sails. Explore. Dream. Discover."

– Mark Twain

My Mom and Dad (Grammy and Bumpa to the grandchildren) moved 14 driving hours away to the west coast of British Columbia in 1979 and later to Bellingham, Washington. My Dad's reasoning for these moves was that instead of sitting in the snow in the winter time, he could sit in the fog and rain of the west coast. Every year, they drove back out to Alberta in May – hoping the last of the snow had been seen - and then returned home in October, preferably before the first snow fell. Even after my Mom passed away a few years ago, my Dad stuck to the May head east and October head west travel schedule.

"Great fathers get promoted to grandfathers"

— **Author: Unknown**

Last year, when he left for the coast, my two sons, Tommy and Davey, came to me and said they were worried about Bumpa driving all of that way at 81 years of age. They felt that the following May, we should fly out to meet him in Seattle and then all drive back together. It is always a great plan when teenage boys want to spend time with their grandfather. However, the plan needed to be 'Bumpa approved'.

A few days later, Tommy and Davey gave Bumpa a call. The conversation was a long one due to the constant repeating of what one just asked or said that occurs when one tries to talk to Bumpa on the phone. But it was worth it. Bumpa eventually agreed to the plan the kids had devised.

I set up an itinerary which included flying to Seattle after the boys finished school on a Friday in May. I planned to run the Tacoma Marathon on Saturday morning. We would then meet up with my brother Bobby and his family Saturday afternoon, and all go to see the baseball game - Seattle Mariners versus Chicago White Sox - Saturday evening. Tommy, Davey and I would drive back to Alberta with Bumpa on the Sunday. The boys would be back in time for school on Monday. What a plan!

When we phoned Bumpa in Bellingham on Christmas day, each and every person in the family, both in Washington and in Alberta, reminded Bumpa of what was going to happen in May. In January, I sent a UPS Express envelope that included some of his mail plus detailed written instructions of the May itinerary. In February, everyone in the family went over everything with Bumpa on the phone again. Then in early April, another UPS Express Envelope was sent to Bumpa with his mail and, once again, written details of the whole itinerary.

All should have been in place, yes?

On Thursday, May 1st, eight days before the "Bumpa" schedule was to kick in, I received an email on my Blackberry from my brother Bobby in Bellingham. He just wanted to let me know that Bumpa left for Alberta early that morning and should be at our house in Lethbridge around 9 pm that evening.

"NO WAY", I said to myself.

The first question that came to mind was why my brother would let Bumpa leave, but the answer was immediate and simple. No one "lets" Bumpa go anywhere. He has always come and gone at the drop of a hat and always on his schedule. Typically, no one in the family knows exactly when he is coming, or when he might be leaving. This time, because of all of the planning and money invested, this was not the time for him to be "drop of the hat". I was not happy.

Sure enough, he arrived around 9 pm to our house in Lethbridge, Alberta. I immediately received "hey guess what? Bumpa is here!" text messages and voicemail from my kids.

I got home two days later on the Sunday afternoon, May 4th and confronted Dad about coming 8 days early when he knew the plan. He said, "I thought I would show everybody that I don't need anyone to drive me anywhere." Followed by, "I don't know where the Seattle Airport is anyway". Even though he has driven past the Seattle Airport for years, Dad argued that he did not know where it was and that he had never seen a sign telling him how to get there. I detailed how much money had been spent on: one-way flights for the three of us; the Marathon entry fee; tickets to the baseball game; two nights of hotel; etc. Then I highlighted the lost opportunity for us to see my brother's family and a major league ball game.

The kitchen in our house went quiet. After a few minutes Bumpa leaned back in his chair, had a sip of his beer and said, "The answer is simple. Just get on that computer thing of yours and book return flights for the three of you. I'll pay the difference." Return flights were about 4 times as much as the original tickets, bought during a seat sale months before. So that wasn't going to work. Plus part of the fun for Tommy and Davey was going to be in travelling with their Bumpa. He was here safe and sound now anyway. I suggested that we just forget the whole thing, eat the costs, and carry on with life.

After many more minutes of silence, he took another sip of his beer and said, "Well I am not doing anything here anyway. It is not like I have any pressing appointments or chores to do. Why don't I just drive back out to Bellingham tomorrow, and we stick to the same game plan as before?" Now there was a stretch outside of normal comfort zone thinking. Keeping in mind that Bellingham is 14 hours of non-stop driving away, I was thinking to myself that it really wasn't that bad of an idea. My younger son Davey immediately piped up that he would go with Bumpa, mentioning that we would defeat the original purpose if Bumpa drove alone. Really, Davey was looking for an excuse to miss a week of school. But, my mind was working. If Bumpa and Davey left early Friday morning, Davey would only miss a half day of school, and then Tommy and I could fly out as planned. Problem solved and the Seattle trip was back on.

On the way to school the next morning, Tommy asked why two people would drive out and two people would fly. He said, "Why not get a credit from Air Canada for all three one-way flights and then all 4 of us drive together?" Why not? So, we made a new plan and I got it "Bumpa approved" when I got back to the house.

Air Canada indeed gave us credit for the flights, to be used within a year. I called Bobby to ensure he knew that everything was back on for the weekend. I reconfirmed with the hotel that everything was good with our rooms (very important as the hotel was right at the start and finish line of the marathon). Bumpa was good to go as he had not really even had a chance to unpack.

The four of us left right after school on Thursday, May 8th and spent the night in Spokane, Washington. We arrived in Tacoma in the early afternoon on Friday and checked into the hotel. We then headed into Seattle to act as tourists for a few hours and find some seafood at a restaurant along the harbour. As we drove north on Interstate #5 from the hotel towards Seattle, Bumpa noticed the signs to the Sea-Tac Airport and announced "hell, I know where the airport is. I have driven past it a bunch of times. In fact, every time I have driven to Alberta." Of course, he had no recollection of the argument a few days before that he didn't know where the airport was.

I ran the marathon bright and early Saturday morning. Bumpa, Tommy and Davey slept in, had breakfast and were just coming out of the hotel to see me finish when I walked in, already finished. We drove back into Seattle and met my brother, my sister-in-law Winnie, my niece Taylor and my nephew Reid, along the Seattle harbour Saturday afternoon. We all went to the baseball game that evening. On Sunday morning, we got up, had a bite to eat, and drove all of the way back to Lethbridge, Alberta.

All was good. We had to stretch outside of our comfort zones and outside of our original plans, but all was good. And the time spent with Bumpa, which was double what had originally been planned, was invaluable.

Comfort zones are people's "cement shoes" to taking risk, missing out on opportunities and generally holding them back from achieving their goals.

> *You don't drown by falling in the water;*
> *you drown by staying there*
>
> — Anonymous

Successful people seem to have an "it is possible" way of thinking – like Bumpa did for the trip to Seattle – and stretching outside of their comfort zones in order to achieve. Successful people kick off their cement shoes or, at the very least, wear a pair that weighs a lot less than the average person's.

Comfort zone dwellers have the talent or the capabilities to achieve all of their goals. Yet, they build an imaginary border and look for the safety and satisfaction in experiences they already know. They stay in their zone – where there is little to no risk and their own personally designed sense of security.

A secure feeling perhaps, but in my experience, comfort zone dwellers are many times the least satisfied because, quite simply, they do not have what they have dreamed about having. Steps towards achieving what they really want are rarely taken. Confidence is highest when there is nothing that might challenge them to move out of their comfort zone. Even though they have dreams and goals that, to be achieved, require "stretching". They are standing in their own way.

There is a way out, a way to stretch, see the success, and gain the confidence to stretch further. How can we all get to that same level?

DANNY DIAMOND SUCCESS TIP:

You have what you have. Everything you have is already inside your current mentally created comfort zone. Most everything that you want, wish for, or have on your goals list, is outside of your current imaginary fenced-off boundaries. If it wasn't, you would already have achieved it. People that don't continuously try to expand their current comfort zone do not grow.

Whether one believes it or not, everyone has the physical capability to stretch and grow – to become uncomfortable. The fastest way to do it is by using your network. Review the network list you created in Chapter #1. If you were honest, open and uninhibited in creating your list, it is loaded with people just itching to help you stretch and achieve. Pick a few out that you feel can help, and utilize them. They have so much experience to share with you.

BEHAVIOUR

Who do you hang out with? How real or fake are you with those you hang out with? How non-committal are you to projects and opportunities? What is your *avoidance* level? These aspects are the most significant in people getting in and staying in their own way to success.

1) Fake, a negative state. These are people who like to hang out with people who are at the same level of stagnation. They like to **blame** for being stuck where they are. They are pretenders every time they aren't doing what is necessary to achieve what they say they want to achieve. They suck life energy out of others around them and hold others back. They try to keep everyone in their network inside *their* comfort zone – where the 'faker's' sense of security lives.

2) Non-committal, refusal to connect. By directing attention away from having to connect to a certain procedure or idea or action, non-committal people are very vague and rarely come clean on how they really feel. They are reluctant to *expose themselves for success*. The lack of commitment and taking the risk to commit holds them back from achieving. Non-committal people are fence sitters, allowing for the option to shrink back into their comfort zone. You are trying to build and utilize a team to achieve more success faster. Non-committers are not team players.

3) Avoidance. When people avoid decision making, or taking steps to capitalize on an opportunity, or participating on a project, it is typically in direct proportion to their confidence level. Remember that a comfort zone dweller's confidence level is highest when events don't take them *outside of their comfort zone*. Due to fear of rejection and negative feedback if they speak up or commit, avoiders let others take the lead. Avoiders are not someone you want to hand the ball to in an important game. Avoiders are worried about criticism and ridicule. Yet, they can be some of the worst at ridiculing, judging or criticizing others, projects or ideas.

Doing nothing is very hard to do...
you never know when you're finished.

— Leslie Nielsen

If you want to achieve certain things but are not taking the steps necessary, you can create new behaviours that support you on your way to success and out of your current comfort zone. The fastest way to gain confidence and support is to expose yourself about the true levels of success you would like to achieve and your network will help you.

BELIEFS

Our belief system starts at an early age from observations of those around us and the level of risk, effort, and mentoring they were willing to accept in order to achieve their goals and desires. We took all of this early information and made our own assumptions on how things are, and how we are, and what expectations we have. Our interpretations of what those around us did and said helped us to form our comfort zones.

The good news is, just like with behaviour, beliefs and values can change over time, allowing you to grow, to stretch and achieve. If your believability factor increases, then your belief system and values will naturally increase.

An example for me was the belief of my grandfather that I could make and play on a baseball team in the city of Lethbridge. He sold me on a possibility and supported me in the "doing". That experience outside of my comfort zone boundaries stretched my belief of what I could achieve.

CONDITIONING

New conditioning from an ever changing environment (school, University or College, career, business, marriage, children, etc.) is "force-change", for lack of a better word, and happens more regularly.

My definitions of conditioning that can limit our success are:

- Advice that you have received, good or bad, past and present, that you decided to accept or act on.
- People you associate with. Successful or unsuccessful? Supportive or unsupportive? Motivated or un-motivated?
- Taking the easy way of doing things, even if the easy way does not attain your dreams and goals.

EXERCISE 6: *Conditioning*

Refer to the networking list you created in Chapter 1.

You created your circles chart with arrows based on who you felt you needed to move closer to in order to achieve more success and those that you needed to move away from.

STEP 1:

As per the following example, create two additional columns on your network list you created in Chapter #1. Title these columns "Good/Bad Advice" and "Wants/Doesn't Want Success".

* Note: a template of this form is available at
www.thecolourofmyunderwearisblue.com

MY NETWORKING OOH LA LA! LIST

Name	Relation/ Category (family, friend, associate, acquaintance, mentor, etc.)	Most influencing aspect of this person	Time in my life of most influence (ex. now; 1995; last year; in school, childhood, etc.)	Provided Good/Bad Advice	Wants Success/ Doesn't Want Success

As you look over your list again, pencil in whether the person gave/gives you good or bad advice. In the last column, make a judgment for each person by asking yourself, "does this person want success and do they want to achieve their dreams?"

As always, go fairly quickly and go with your instinct as that is what will be the most right for you.

STEP 2:

After completing Step 1, take a look at those that you said you wanted to move closer to and those that you said you needed to distance yourself from in order to attain greater success.

Does there need to be any adjustments in the directions of arrows, as well as any revisions to your final list of supporters? If so, make those changes now.

Please note that you may decide certain people in your network are worth moving towards because of a certain goal you are looking to achieve; yet they might not be the ones you would move closer to for some other specific goal.

For example, the guys I curled competitively with were fellows I would have indicated as moving closer to in the exercise in Chapter 1, for the goal of winning a Provincial Curling Championship. However, for attaining a qualifying time for the Boston Marathon, I would have indicated other people, runners in my network, as needing to move closer to. For business goals, yet another group of people in my network would be indicated as needing to move closer to.

Therefore, as you make any changes to your list and who you need to move closer to and move away from, you can make it as goal specific as you desire.

STEP 3:

The last part of my definition of conditioning, taking the easy way out, is something you have to look within for.

The questions to ask yourself are:

"Do I take the easy way out of a situation, project, job, or assignment?"

_____ Yes   _____ No

"Does my answer above support me on my way to success and achievement of my goals?"

_____ Yes   _____ No

PROCRASTINATION
– A DEADLY SUCCESS/ACHIEVEMENT KILLER.

I am getting ready to commence to start tomorrow.

– Zig Ziglar

The sooner I fall behind, the more time I have to catch up.

— Author Unknown

There is much written about the psychology behind procrastination but I do know that, typically, procrastinators are not lazy. In fact, when it gets to deadline time and their backs are against the wall, most procrastinators can really turn it on. The problem is that they have left the completion of a task or project far too long. It is not that they are unable or unwilling to do the work. Their comfort level is simply to defer, postpone, or find excuses to delay.

*You know you are getting old when it takes
too much effort to procrastinate.*

- Author Unknown

All of the procrastinators I know are poor at setting goals, reluctant to set goals, or have never set any goals. They do not have a plan or direction in place that they can control to the best of their ability. Their comfort zone is to wait for things to come at them - both work related and personal - which creates the opportunity to defer them to a later time. All the while other things come at them and build a back log.

I also find that procrastinators have a difficult time asking others for help. They are "doers" and part of feeling overwhelmed and the need to postpone comes from the fact that they intend to do the work themselves.

The fastest way to change procrastination tendencies is to utilize one's network. There are people in everyone's network who are experts at setting goals, planning and prioritizing commitments. There are people in everyone's network who will help and support with learning to delegate. Many times, there are people in the network who will actually take on some of the workload and commitments themselves. They just need to be asked.

Break the procrastination comfort zone boundaries. Take action instead of deferring or delaying. Experiencing firsthand the success and feeling of achievement that can be accomplished by utilizing the support of your network,

The best way to get something done is to begin.

— Author Unknown

Like everything else that works in cycles, there are times that successful people are very comfortable in their comfort zone. They have plateaued, so to speak.

My experience has been that the plateau effect does not last for long for successful people. Complacency, a success killer, is not high on the list for someone that is used to stretching outside of their comfort zone and getting results. When you have stretched your boundaries and experienced the attainment of those goals and desires, it breeds more action and drive to continue to stretch, to attain more. Success breeds success.

Let's look at some graphical representation of comfort zones. As you work through these exercises, please keep in mind that:

Successful people do not Justify

Justification is just a way to declare oneself free of responsibility. Successful people look in the mirror everyday and take full responsibility for everything that is happening to them, good and not so good.

Successful people create an environment for growth and achievement.

They don't set limits. Even though they recognize that there will be obstacles along the way, they don't allow obstacles to act as roadblocks. Obstacles simply become opportunities waiting to happen.

Successful people know that when stretching one's borders, there is not the usual "safe zone".

A safe zone can't exist if success is to be attained. Successful people are always working on their belief/values and conditioning to allow themselves to grow.

Successful people know that it has to be fun along the way.

Moving forward is fun. Taking action is fun. Attaining is fun. Achieving is fun. If you have ever been around anyone who has lost some weight or gotten back into shape through dedication and discipline; you know how much energy they have and how inspiring they are to others. They stopped talking about it and took action. Action wins out over everything.

Successful people know that it is important to utilize their network every step along the way – to *expose themselves for success*.

They utilize their network for planning, for support, for encouragement, for mentoring, for increasing the believability factor, for breaking through to new levels.

EXERCISE 7: *The Success Graph*

* Note: a template of this graph is available at www.thecolourofmyunderwearisblue.com

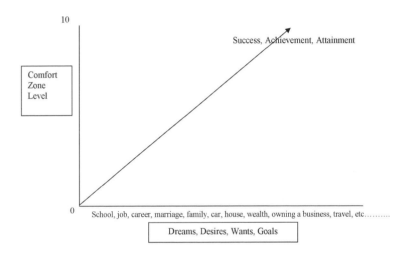

1. The success/achievement/attainment arrow is always moving upwards. It is calling for a need for the comfort zone level to always increase. The road to success is about continuously stretching the comfort zone.

2. Decide on a scale of 0-10 where you feel your current comfort level is.

Level 0 means that you are the consummate Faker, Non-committer and Avoider.

Level 10 means you fear nothing and nothing is too big for you to tackle.

Decide what level fits you and draw a horizontal line across to the success/achievement arrow line. Then draw a line straight down to the "Dreams, Desires, Wants, Goals" line.

This is your current comfort zone box.

3. Now, write inside the comfort zone box all that you have attained (possessions, etc.), all the goals that have been reached and all that you have achieved to date (awards, education, etc.). Remember, everything you have is already inside your current comfort zone box. Write them all down and remember nothing achieved is too small.

Your graph may now look something like this:

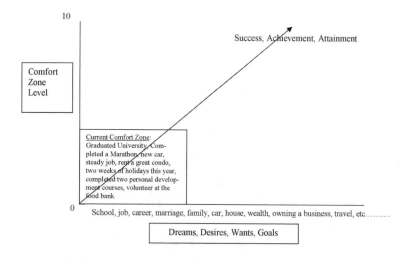

4. Everything you want and desire is outside your current comfort zone box. If you have never made a dreams or goals list, now is the time. Take a blank piece of paper and, working on the basis of unlimited time and money, write down all that you want to have, experience and contribute.

5. Indicate on the graph how much you feel you would have to expand your comfort zone in order to attain the items you listed in step 4 above. Please note that your comfort zone will have to expand only a small amount in order to achieve some of the items on your list. Your comfort zone will have to expand significantly more in order to achieve other dreams and desires.

Decide for yourself how much you would like to expand from your current comfort zone level, at this time.

As before, draw a line over to the success/achievement line, then draw a line straight down to the "Dreams, Desires, Wants, Goals" line. This is your desired or *stretched* comfort zone box, necessary to achieve some of the items you listed.

Now write in all of the things you think you would attain or accomplish if you did indeed stretch yourself as far as you have indicated. There is no right or wrong because, as mentioned previously, this is you talking to you. You can change it at anytime.

Your new graph may now look something like this:

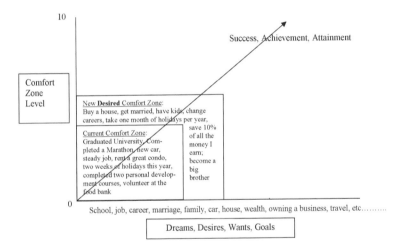

6. You can do the above exercise as many times as you like and add as many levels as you feel are necessary to accomplish items on your dreams and goals list.

You now have a graphical representation of *your comfort zone*.

It is my belief that everyone has the ability to succeed and your "self-disclosure" in these exercises is a huge step towards multiple successes for you. The only thing missing for most people is the 'doing' - the taking action part.

In my experience, the level of action taking is what makes the successful person's comfort zone box larger than others. "Action" is what creates such a wide variety of success levels in our society.

> *"Sometimes it is the little things you do that can make a difference. What one thing can you do today that will make you more effective and lead you toward your goal? Take action now!"*
>
> —Bob Proctor, Personal Development Guru,
> Author and star of the movie "The Secret".

The next action item on this journey is identifying:

- *who* in your network could help you right away with specific goals and desires you wrote down; and

- *exposing* yourself and your plans to them.

These individuals are chomping at the bit to help you in any way they can.

Expose yourself for success.

As my great mentor Mr. Ralph Askar, the President and CEO of Instant Imprints always says, "**are we gonna do it, or are we just gonna talk about it?**"

CHAPTER 4:

— Maximum Exposure —

"It's not what you know but who you know that makes the difference."

— Anonymous

 DANNY DIAMOND SUCCESS TIP:

It's not just who you know, but who they are and how much you ask for and utilize their knowledge and expertise that makes *all* of the difference.

It was a hot summer day in Barons, Alberta Canada – Paradise - in 1968. I was 10 years old. My best buddy at the time and I had explored around town for most of the day. We returned to my house in the afternoon for a glass of water. While snooping around the kitchen, we found some matches. Suddenly, what had been a good day turned into a great day. 10 year olds with matches. What could be better?

Our house sat on 10 vacant acres considered in the county for tax purposes, but was really inside the natural border of our small town.

With the matches in hand, my buddy and I hurried outside and behind our garage. Taking turns lighting a couple and watching them burn down to our finger tips, we would blow them out at the last second and let them drop into the grass. Each time reminding one another to throw them into the burning barrel at the edge of our driveway to remove proof and ensure the "not getting caught" part. In those days, people burned their garbage in a 45 gallon drum with pickup provided by the village.

Eventually just watching a match burn does not have enough excitement, at least not for a couple of 10 year-olds. Bunching up a few pieces of dried grass and burning those became boring rather quickly as well. We came to the conclusion that we could probably burn something bigger and better, and still not get caught. The decision was made to check out what was in our garage which, in those days, my father used for storage only.

Our garage, about 10 yards southeast of our house, was an old wooden building, painted white, with an oiled wooden floor and insulated with straw. I didn't go into the garage much. The old wooden doors were hard to open and close. The times I did go inside, I remember there was a unique smell and atmosphere made up of the mustiness, the oiled floor, and the daylight coming from the one window in the back. There were countless valuable things stored in our garage. What I remember most was the old antique phonograph that still worked perfectly, my dad's fishing gear, and his goose hunting decoys.

Once inside, we searched for something that we could burn and stumbled upon a plastic one gallon jug that was about half full of gasoline. The day just kept getting better - 10 years old, matches and now gasoline. The two of us discussed what the best procedure would be. It was decided that lighting a spot of gasoline on the floor was better than burning something else, like a piece of paper, because there would be less smoke. It sure sounded logical at the time.

Rock, paper, scissors were used to determine who got to light the match. I won. We dribbled a few drops of gas on the floor of the garage (did I mention that it was an oiled, wooden floor?) and set the jug of gas a couple of feet away. As soon as I lit the one and only match we had the opportunity to light, and touched the spot of gasoline on the floor, we immediately discovered that there were drips that had followed the jug of gas all the way back to the place we had set it in. What happened next was a flash in time but it seemed to be in slow motion for me – perhaps just so I could get the lesson fully. The flame from the spot on the floor I had put the match on, jumped quickly to the next spot and the next spot and so on. Then the flame jumped onto the jug of gasoline itself. The outside of the jug caught on fire immediately and, 10 years old or not, we knew what would be coming next when the flames reached the gasoline on the inside of the jug.

My friend and I instinctively ran outside as fast as we could. Opening the big, usually hard to open garage door did not pose a problem when running scared for our lives. My buddy kept running all the way past our house, down our driveway and, I assume, to his house down the street. For just a few seconds, I stood there with a terrible empty feeling in the pit of my stomach, wishing I could take it all back. I ran inside the house yelling that the garage was on fire. My Mother took one look out the kitchen window and called it in.

In a village of 200 people, the fire department is all volunteers. When the fire siren would go off, the speed with which the men in town took action was remarkable. They came running from everywhere.

My Mom questioned me to ensure that no one was in the garage. I remember trying to convince myself that the gasoline had simply burned itself out and that there really was no real fire. That hope disappeared when I went back outside and saw that our neighbour to the south had grabbed our garden hose and was trying his best to fight the fire which, with an oiled floor and straw insulation, was spreading fast. By the time the fire engine arrived in our driveway it was hopeless. The fire fighters sprayed water on the garage but mainly sprayed down the roof of our house to ensure that the fire did not make a jump.

The smoke billowed for everyone to see from miles away. Most everyone in town was standing in our yard and driveway. A fire is big news in a small town. Cars were parked up and down the street in front of our house. That is when my Dad drove into town from the east after having delivered fuel to some farms in the area. He probably saw the smoke from miles away. Now he could see all of the activity in his yard and, I am sure, he could see what was left of his garage. I quickly went through a list of possible excuses I could use to keep from getting perhaps the worst punishment I was ever to receive. I mean if you could get in trouble for doing normal bad things, what might be the punishment for burning down the garage?

Then my buddy showed up. Just as I was starting to go through my list of excuses for his opinion and validation, my Mother spotted us. She stepped towards us with her finger pointed and her voice raised. My supposedly best buddy immediately announced to my Mom that it was me who had stolen the matches, me who had found the gasoline jug and me who had actually lit the match that caused the fire. Then I watched him run off back home again. Luckily for me, with so many people around, my mother chose not to give me the complete tongue lashing she probably wanted to. I was told I would get it later.

The garage didn't quite burn to the ground. Partial walls stayed up and even the roof stayed intact for the most part. The firemen ensured that the garage remains were soaked through. A few of the firefighters and some of our neighbours stayed into the evening for some supper and a drink with my parents. I never did get punished - at least not a "licken" as I was expecting. My Mother explained that sometimes we do things that are so bad the punishment is the realization of what we have taken from someone else.

My brother Jimmy, some of the other kids in town and me helped my Dad tear down the remains of the garage. Then Dad built a new one. It was on a cement foundation and the garage itself was built totally of metal. Roof, walls, large door, side door – everything was metal. One of Don Lyon's kids was never going to burn down the garage again.

Fast forward 35 years to September, 2003. I was in the Lost Soul 100-mile Ultra Marathon in Lethbridge, Alberta, Canada. One of the toughest "ultras" anywhere, the 100-mile race is three laps of the course. My son Tommy, then 11 years old, had received special permission from the race organizers months before to enter the 50 Kilometre Ultra

Marathon race, which was one lap of the same course. If successful, Tommy would become the youngest in Western Canada to complete an ultra-marathon. Tommy's 50 kilometre race started 23 hours after the start of my 100-miler. As it worked out, the timing was such that I finished lap number 2, after running through the night, just about the same time Tommy started his race. I arrived at the headquarter aid station tent in time to wish him good luck and see him take off with about 100 other runners. Although Connie and I had some concerns, the other runners were absolutely amazing in their support for Tommy.

I weighed in and had my blood pressure checked and then headed out on Leg 1 of the final lap. Tommy ran slowly and I caught up to him waiting on the hillsides of Leg 2. We were able to run together for the rest of the day, making it a very special race for me. Tommy's constant banter and his questions on almost every subject imaginable to man probably did more to help me keep moving forward than any of my training leading up to the race.

At the second last aid station with about 8 miles, or 13 kilometres, left to go for both of us, Tommy and I collapsed into lawn chairs. I had been out on the course for about 33 hours and Tommy 10 hours. The Lost Soul Ultra-Marathon volunteers, the best in any race I have ever been in, were getting us some water before we headed back out. All of our family, including my Dad, were there to support us at the aid station. I had been fighting blisters on my feet since lap number 2 and had a nasty one on the heel of my left foot. There is always great debate amongst those in the running community whether it is better to pop a blister, or tape it and leave it be. Following a volunteer's advice we had just been taping it with duct tape at every aid station to try and keep it from ripping open. As I removed my shoe, sock and the duct tape at the aid station the blister was now full of juice and huge. At that point in the race, I changed my mind and decided that I wanted it popped.

A request for a pin or a needle was made to the aid station volunteers. Before they could act, my Dad proudly announced that he had a pin in his change purse. What my Dad carries with him – in his pockets, in his change purse, on the old pouch he used to wear on his belt - is almost folklore for anyone who has ever witnessed his "Johnny on the spot" capabilities of carrying what most of us would consider junk or needless. Proud that he had provided an immediate solution, Dad studied the situation carefully, almost as if he was admiring how big the blister had gotten and that it was ready to explode. I raised my foot up as best I could so that he could see it clearly and didn't have to bend over too far.

Instead of sticking the pin into the blister in kind of a parallel to my skin motion, Dad stuck it in perpendicular, as in a right angle, right through the blister and right into my heel. He jabbed it straight in, fast and hard, and I went straight up. As I let out a yell in pain, along with a few unrepeatable adjectives, my son Tommy, 11 years old and absolutely dead tired, very calmly leaned over and said to me, "that was for burning down the garage".

MAXIMUM EXPOSURE

The UPS Store Franchisee Jeff Parker has a great line that goes something like this, "you can have the best idea in the world, but if you don't tell anyone about it, it doesn't mean anything". In other words, no one can help you with it and no one can support you around the idea, including customers, if it is not "exposed" to them.

 DANNY DIAMOND SUCCESS TIP:

Stealing from Jeff Parker's quote: You can have the best ideas, the best plans, the best goals and dreams; but if no one knows about them, they don't mean anything.

I bring up Jeff because his quote about ideas is the exact same as dealing with

"Exposing yourself to your network" and "exposing yourself for success". If you don't tell anyone about it, if you don't share, if you don't expose yourself, no one can help you and no one can support you in whatever you are trying to accomplish.

So my challenge to everyone is to take that great network list you created in Chapter 1, and tweaked in Chapters 2 and 3, and start sharing your successes, ideas, goals, and desires with those on the list.

 DANNY DIAMOND SUCCESS TIP:

"Expose Yourself For Success".

Show those on your network list the *colour of your underwear* (figuratively speaking of course). Provide them with maximum exposure on your ideas, plans, goals and dreams, and let them help accelerate your accomplishments and achievements on the road to success.

I believe that community is the real description of one's network..

Community is described as (from the Merriam-Webster Online Dictionary)

- A unified body of individuals
- People with common interests, supporting each other
- An interacting population of various kinds of individuals
- A body of persons having common history or common interests

It is easy to define Barons, Alberta, Canada – Paradise - as a community because it was a village with borders. However, the physical town itself was only a small part of the community. The real community was the people inside.

"There can be no vulnerability without risk; there can be no community without vulnerability; there can be no peace, and ultimately no life, without community."

—M. Scott Peck

Times may change but the characteristics of the road to success and the community we build around ourselves are still the same and have always been the same. That is why the work you did in the first 3 chapters is so important. You identified your community, and your successes, and comfort level within it.

Real success comes from what you do for and with others, as opposed to "what's in it for me". Unfortunately, we human beings just seem to be wired with ego high on the list of attributes. Ironically, at least in my experience, the "what's in it for me" part – the gains, the success, the money, or whatever it is – comes automatically when ego is set aside. When contribution is your priority, success accelerates very quickly.

EXERCISE 8:

Refer to the two exercises in the last chapter.

Combining the newly revised Networking Ooh La, La! list in Exercise 6 with the new comfort zone boxes you created in Exercise 7, you should be able to identify who in your network you could utilize to help you **right away** with the specific goals and desires you wrote down.

Step 1 - Write down one of the goals outside your current comfort zone from Exercise 7.

Step 2 – From Exercise 6 (your revised Networking Ooh La La! list) write down the person or persons who you feel could help you with the goal listed in Step 1 above. .

Step 3 - Make a commitment to contact them.

Step 4 - *Expose yourself* and your plans to them. **Expose yourself for success.**

Step 5 – Repeat Step 1 thru 4 for the next goal or desire that you indicated in Exercise 7 as being outside your current comfort zone. Do at least 5 goals or desires and if you can do more, great.

Example:

Goal/Desire 1 (step 1): **Buy a house**

Person(s) who can help with this (step 2)	I will contact by (step 3)	3 things I will share (expose) about my goal and desire. (step 4)
1. Joe Smith (mortgage broker)	The end of this month.	1. I want to buy a house within the next 90 days 2. How much money I have saved for a down payment 3. How much I can afford for a mortgage payment
2. Jane Melling (investment manager)	Next week	1. The need to sell some of my stock portfolio for the down payment and the timing for tax purposes 2. The need to continue to build my stock/mutual fund investment plan even though I am buying a house. 3. If I were more attentive to my investments and your advice, would my returns be higher?
3. Patsy Sately (realtor)	tomorrow	1. Range of houses I can afford 2. Areas of town preferred 3. Request for any demographic studies she may be able to provide.
4. Friends and family	Friday night	1. Type and size of house I am interested in. 2. The areas of town looked at 3. Since this is my first house, any ideas on what to look out for
5. Business Colleagues	Starting tomorrow	1. I am working on buying house 2. Anyone selling theirs 3. Anyone selling any furniture, appliances, etc.

Following is a chart you can print off for each goal and desire for Exercise 8.

* Note: a template of this form is available at www. thecolourofmyunderwearisblue.com

Goal/Desire: _____

Person(s) who can help with this (step 2)	I will contact by (step3)	Three things I will share (expose) about my goal and desire. (step 4)
1.		1. 2. 3.
2.		1. 2. 3.
3.		1. 2. 3.

4.		1.
		2.
		3.
5.		1.
		2.
		3.

I believe everyone has the ability to achieve everything they want and desire. All they need to do is ask for help by *exposing* those wants and desires. That is what you are creating in Exercise 8 above.

Don't wait to use your network.

Take your completed sheets from Exercise 8 and run full speed ahead with them.

Congratulations on being an action taker.

CHAPTER 5:

– *Same Old, Same Old* –

**A situation or someone's behaviour remains
the same as it always has.**

*"We do the things we do because we are the way we learned to
be. And the way we have always done it - the same old, same old
- is easiest. If we really want to change our ways we can. It is our
choice because it is just a re-learning (or an unlearning)."*

— **Danny Lyon**

**Get out of the Same Old, Same Old.
Make everything about your life vibrant.**

After a year hiatus, in 1985 I decided to come out of "retirement"
and play another year of baseball with the Calgary Bears. I was 27 that
year. With great guys on the team, the focus was going to be more on fun
than hard core competitive baseball.

In the first game of the year I was pitching against lead-off hitter Rick, a former team mate and who had played on a scholarship at a University in the U.S. After I warmed up, our catcher came out to the mound to get the signals. I had three pitches – fastball, curve, and what I called a "screwball" which, as a left-handed pitcher, broke down and away from right-handed batters. Our catcher settled in behind the plate and Rick stepped up. "One" for a fastball and Rick let it go for strike one. Next pitch, "two" for a curve, and Rick swung and missed for strike two. "Three" for a screwball was signalled. Remember I said it was supposed to break down and away from a right-handed batter? Rick was a right-handed batter. Unfortunately, this particular screwball *forgot* it was supposed to break down and away. It just sat there. Rick hit it so hard and so far it might still be rolling. As Rick circled the bases and thanked me for the "gift", our catcher came out to tell me that not only were we not going to use the screwball the rest of that game, perhaps he would never call it again for the rest of the season.

We had a good season and made it to the Provincial Championships.

1985 was my last year as a player and my second year as a baseball umpire. The previous year I did not play baseball at all and umpiring seemed to go quite well. I really enjoyed it. I soon learned how challenging it could be to do something new (umpiring), while still trying to hold onto what is the most comfortable (playing).

The American Legion Lethbridge Elks hosted a very popular international tournament each year. The showcase team was from Taiwan, along with teams from California and Nevada, attracting a lot of media attention and drawing large crowds. My first game in the 1985 tournament, I umpired on the bases. For game two, between the Nevada and California teams, I was behind the plate.

In the 1st inning the shortstop for California, their best and highly scouted player, stepped out of the batter's box and loudly criticized the strike I had just called on him. Mistake #1 was not reacting, as ball and strike criticism is not normally tolerated. Instead, I remember analyzing in my mind if I would be able to get this guy out if I was the one pitching to him. I was thinking like a player.

In the 4th inning, he did the exact same thing, stepping out to criticize a strike. Mistake #2 was not reacting again. I noticed that I was really into this game, thinking more like the one throwing, hitting, and running the bases, as opposed to calling the game.

In the 6th inning, the California shortstop stepped out after a pitch and this time criticized, not a strike, but a "ball". I had never experienced a batter actually criticizing a call that was in their favour. This guy was criticizing just to criticize and was needlessly delaying the game I was watching (and not necessarily umpiring). This time I ordered him to "shut it" and get back into the batter's box; which he did immediately. The problem was, I used a couple of inappropriate adjectives to really get my point across. As he stepped up to the plate and started to take a practice swing, we both realized at the same time what I had just said.

In the blink of an eye he was in my face to challenge me for cursing. What I could have or should have done was to toss him out of the game – and all probably would have been good. But really, I was in the wrong. I had not stopped the criticism earlier in the game and I had indeed cursed in this incidence. With him in my face, I brought my hands up to his shoulders to reclaim my space and encourage him to get back into the batter's box. As soon as contact with the player was made the manager for California shot out of the dugout. Now I had them both in my face.

I took my verbal lumps from both of them and tried to get the game started again. The manager was very aggressive, relentless and wanted me to toss him out. So I did. Unfortunately, I am left-handed and he thought I would make the signal with my right hand, as any other umpire would. Just as I threw out my left arm and started the "you're out 'a here" motion we have all seen on TV so many times, the manager leaned forward. My little finger hooked his glasses and sent them flying. At the same time, the left shoulder pad of my chest protector went across his forehead and cut him just above his right eye. As with any head cut, there was lots of blood right away.

Now the whole thing was out of control. Their bench emptied and with both the manager and the shortstop leading the mob scene, they pinned me against the backstop. My partner umpire on the bases was trying his best to push the players back. Finally, I yelled to the bloodied California manager, that if he did not leave, I would throw out his whole team one by one. He yelled something back and I signalled (with my right hand this time) that the shortstop was gone. Realizing I was serious and that things had gotten out of control, the manager eventually got his team back into the dugout. Then he and the shortstop left the field.

My partner and I took a few minutes to regain composure. It felt like everyone else in the ball park did the same thing. I was wishing we could just call it a day and get out of there.

A replacement batter was announced and we finally settled in for the first pitch to restart the game. It was a ball in the dirt well before home plate - an obvious "ball" to everyone in the stadium. The Nevada coach shot out of his dugout. I should have tossed him before he took two steps towards me. Shaken from the near riot a few minutes earlier and having not been in umpire mode for most of the game, I let him come all the way out. He got in my face and gave me another lecture on balls and strikes and giving calls to the other team because of the riff the other team had just created.

The game now could not get over fast enough for me and it seemed to take hours to finish the last 3 innings.

In the umpire's room afterwards, I talked with some of the other umpires about losing control of a game. I thought long and hard about ever stepping out on the field as an umpire again. Being a player was much easier. The other umpires encouraged me to stick it out for at least the rest of the tournament – much like getting back on your bicycle when falling off. In addition, one of the Tournament Organizers informed me of the complications I would create to the umpire schedule if I did not fulfill my commitment. I felt stuck.

I did come back the next day only to be greeted by a Policeman in the umpire's room. The parent's of the California shortstop had filed a complaint for swearing in the presence of a minor. The policeman took my statement. He said that there would be no further action from the police and disciplinary action, if any, would come from American Legion baseball or the Tournament committee.

I sat alone in the umpire's room for a long time, convincing myself that this was the end of umpiring for me. I was watching the game instead of umpiring it. I had sworn at a minor. I broke the glasses of the manager and cut his forehead. I had lost control of the game. A near riot had broken out. A legal complaint had been filed against me. I was convinced that there would be disciplinary action from the Tournament Committee. I decided I would meet my commitment for the rest of the weekend and then quit umpiring.

Quitting was easiest. The same old, same old – being a player – was easiest.

In came my umpire partner from the day before. He informed me that the game we were doing in a few minutes involved the same California team, with me behind home plate calling balls and strikes again. Before I could express my reservations, he offered to umpire home plate (even though he did not do home plate very often). Wow, what a relief and what support for me. Then the Tournament Director and two of the committee members came into the umpire's room. Waiting for the worst, I was surprised when they informed me that they had met with the California and Nevada teams. Both teams were told that if there were any more problems in their games, they would be asked to leave the tournament immediately. More support. Confident compared to just 30 minutes before, I stepped onto the field and stood near the first base dugout. The national anthems were about to be played when the California manager came over to me and apologized for what had happened the day before. I apologized as well.

Feeling much better and humbled by everyone's support, I completed that tournament. I quit being a player after that year, and I kept umpiring right up until I started travelling out of the country with my work.

Getting out of the Same Old, Same Old is challenging. I thought failure had occurred and my instinct was to retreat back to what I knew best. Then I found out that there was lots of support from my network (more than we know many times) for the new challenge and a breakthrough occurred.

The diagram below demonstrates what happens when we take on a new direction out of the Same Old, Same Old, and obstacles get in the way. Examples may be losing weight, getting in shape, trying for a raise at work, changing careers, starting a new business, renovating; buying a house; or even becoming an umpire.

The horizontal line represents you on the journey toward a new goal or new direction you have decided to take to improve or enhance your personal, career or business life. Somewhere along the way, obstacles get in the path and the energy will bounce back. How you react at that point in time determines your success of breaking through, or remaining stuck. This is the time that utilization of your network is crucial. In the umpiring example, my network - my umpire partner, the Tournament committee, and even the manager for the California team - came through to help me stay in the game. By fully *exposing* your goals and the challenges slowing you down, your network will come through for you too.

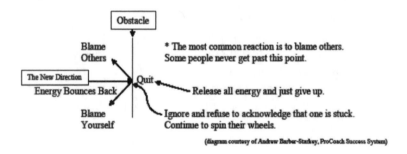

(diagram courtesy of Andrew Barber-Starkey, ProCoach Success System)

The diagram is about Life, Work, and Business. Any time we try to "break out", glitches happen along the way.

Is it better to fall back into the Same Old, Same Old, as I was willing to do by giving up umpiring? Or is striving forward and looking for solutions, the better way to go?

In my experience there is only one direction a successful person takes and that is the cycle of **start – obstacle – breakthrough**. Indeed, do get out of the Same Old, Same Old. Face all and any challenges. Use discipline, commitment and your network until you breakthrough. Then pick something else and go forward again.

> *"Get a goal, get some desire and you'll*
> *have all of the energy you need."*
>
> —Bob Proctor

Breaking through obstacles is not the norm for the majority of people. Most like the path of least resistance. Growth and success rarely come via the path of least resistance.

One of the ways we allow ourselves to get into the rut of the Same Old, Same Old is being busy with life. There are family schedules, personal schedules, work schedules, bills to pay, etc. We develop things to a "can almost handle it" level, the Same Old, Same Old zone if you will, by letting our lives, business, or work rule us instead of the other way around. The motivation to take anything to the next level is put on the back burner as the path of least resistance, what we are already familiar with, takes over.

People love to focus on the obstacles rather than the opportunities. Mention opportunities and they will add in the "buts", and the "whys" something cannot be done, highlighting or inventing the obstacles.

Human nature is to lean towards the negative or the Victim Mode in most situations. When confronted as to why goals are not being reached, the most common reaction is to blame others and listing the excuses as to why things happen TO them.

"Our attitudes control our lives. Attitudes are a secret power working 24 hours a day, for good or bad. It is of paramount importance that we know how to harness and control this great force."

—Tom Blandi

"A pessimist is one who feels bad when he feels good for fear he'll feel worse when he feels better."

—*Unknown*

Blame - to hold responsible; to find fault with; to place responsibility with.

Blaming is an excuse; a passing of the buck; a diversion from having to look in the mirror. Excuses can build on excuses and the fault for lack of desired achievement becomes everyone else and everything else.

"Blamers" are everywhere. In business, owners may blame vendors, suppliers, the franchise, staff, the economy, the Landlord, and they even blame the customers for not reaching desired sales levels. In people's careers, blame can be directed at other departments, department heads, co-workers, head office, upper management, vendors, the economy, work schedules and even customers for not getting the desired position or pay scale. In their personal lives "blamers" direct blame at the weather, their schedule, team mates, the referee, the coach, family members, their job, the bank, teachers, and they even blame their friends for not attaining what they want. It's always something else or someone else, never them.

Complain - to express resentment or displeasure.

Self-sabotaging, complaining is the main road block to personal, career and business success. Since it is a "downer", negative emotion, complaining is the fastest way to disconnect from – **turn-off** - those that could and would help you. Complaining diminishes your network support power. You become unattractive and what comes out of your mouth becomes unattractive. About the only things you do attract are more things to complain about and other negative, complaining people. Complainers think that they have lots to complain about because things aren't going as planned. In reality, the flip side is true. Things aren't happening for them because pretty much all they do is complain.

> *"When you are complaining, you become a living, breathing crap magnet."*
>
> – T. Harv Eker, Author of #1 NY Times Bestseller
> *Secrets of the Millionaire Mind*

Justify – to demonstrate to be right, or valid; to declare free of blame.

If blaming and complaining are the negatives that stall success and getting out of the Same Old, Same Old to move forward, then justification is the negative that defines why the "blames" and "complains" must be true. Justifiers explain their situation – poor performance, out of shape, lack of success, defeat, overweight, etc. – by using other examples. 'I might have failed the test but many in the class did.' 'My business is not doing that well but there are others not doing any better.' 'I would be doing better but the economy is pulling me down.' 'I would have played better but no one was having a good game.'

Justification ties the blaming and complaining together and ensures that any desire to look in the mirror and take responsibility is diverted or delayed for as long as possible.

Blame, complain, and justify, become "The Story". "Your Story". And "Your Story" tells all. It becomes your trademark.

Think about it for a moment. What does your story tell right now? Want to find out?

Just ask your network. They know. You have told it to them many times. If you come from the victim mentality - blame, complain, justify - they know your story all too well. Blame, complain and justify are negatives, making "The Story" negative and ensuring the people attracted to it, attracted to you, are also negative.

Since you made the story up, you can change it anytime. It requires a long hard look in the mirror and making the conscious decision to take full responsibility – for everything. Until you do that, your story won't change.

THE OTHER SIDE

The breakthrough side is the "Victor" side. People on the breakthrough side find a way to make things happen **FOR them, not TO them**.

We have been influenced by everyone in our support network from the time we are first born in helping us perceive, discover, and learn. The best part is, we are still influenced by everyone in our support network now. This means that we have added, adapted, changed and even manipulated beliefs around family, religion, school, money and success all the way along. Meaning we have the power to add, adapt, change and manipulate beliefs now and anytime in our lives.

To breakthrough more obstacles, one of the first steps is to take a look at your beliefs around personal, career and business success. Then, write down exactly what you want to have; to experience; and to contribute to in your life. "Expose" your findings to your network because, typically, those in your network believe more in you and your abilities than you do. Your support network can help you get in alignment with your beliefs, old and new, for maximum success, achievement and satisfaction.

Expose yourself, and the why and the how of breaking through obstacles will take care of itself.

There are great seminars and workshops out there that can help you discover your beliefs, help you change what might be limiting beliefs and add core beliefs that serve you better. Here is an exercise that doesn't take long that works well for me and may get you moving forward sooner.

EXERCISE 9: *Belief*

On a blank sheet of paper write, "**I believe in**…" at the top.

Then just start writing.

Stimulators: I believe in…"honesty, integrity, being responsible for my actions, religion, family, my children, marriage, truth, hard work, school, studying hard, discipline, determination, dedication, faithfulness, loyalty, being a lifetime learner, helping others; volunteering; donating money; serving others…"

Just start writing. Don't think too much.

It is fast and it is fun to do. And you will feel good afterwards.

EXERCISE 10:
Have, Experience, Contribute

Next, on the same or a different sheet of paper write, "**I want to have…**"

Again, just start writing. Don't think too much. You can always add to the list or edit it later.

Stimulators might be: I want to have…"good health, happy kids, a luxury car; a large house with a view; a maid; a fit and lean body; more money than I can spend; a boat; the respect of my peers; great marks in school; a masters degree; a long, satisfying life; unlimited free time to travel; unlimited free time to spend supporting others…"

Next, on the same or a different sheet of paper write, "**I want to experience…**"

I want to experience…"a trip around the world; graduating; seeing my kids graduate; the Boston Marathon; the satisfaction of a life well done; the pyramids; the Great Wall of China; the Australia Gold Coast; love; the love of my family; my successes and goals…"

Next, on the same or a different sheet of paper write, "**I want to contribute to…**"

I want to contribute to…"peace on earth; love of friends and family; a worthy cause; other's success…"

STOP!!!!!

Many of you reading this did exactly that – read. And read only.

Go back and don't just read. Do it. Do the exercises.

They are simple enough and fast enough they can be done anywhere. At the kitchen table, in the living room, at work, on a plane, in a vehicle - wherever you are reading this.

Please do them. Take 5 minutes and do the exercises.

Go ahead. I'll wait...
....
....
....

Thank you.

And there you have it. Your lists.

Doesn't it already feel like you are moving through obstacles?

Doesn't it feel like you are moving away from the Same Old, Same Old?

EXERCISE 11:

Share your lists with your support network.

Expose yourself. The more you do, the more help you will get, the more successful you will become.

Make a commitment to yourself right now to share with someone in your network.

I, _____ , hereby commit to sharing my lists created in the
(your name)

exercises above with the following three people from my Networking Ooh La! La! list:

_____ , _____ ,

_____ ,

by _____ , 20____ .
       (date)

_____

     (your signature)

Now that you have your list and you have some support let's take another look at the obstacles diagram in a bit of a different way, and see how we can always be working towards the breakthroughs and growth areas.

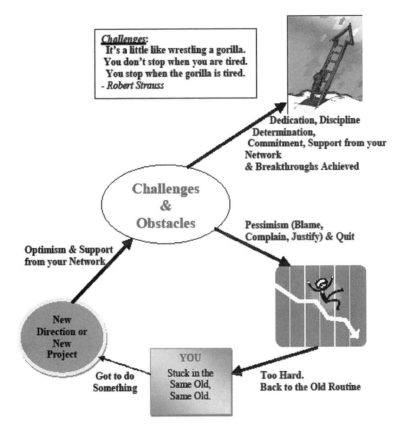

We all go through cycles of achievement followed by obstacles and dips along the way. The idea is to make the dips less each cycle so that the overall gain is exponential. The bottom right of the diagram, returning right back to where we were by quitting, is the least desired but one of the most common pitfalls in achievement.

One thing that helps move the bar higher and keep dips on the way to success at a minimum is the "See the Light" believability factor. Each time you experience a success by "breaking through obstacles" or seeing what others in your network have achieved, the believability of what is possible increases. Two great examples of "See the Light" believability are:

1. The breaking of the 4 minute mile by Roger Bannister in 1954. Once thought unattainable, as soon as Bannister broke the mark with a 3:59.4 finish, others did the same soon after, because the impossible was now possible.

2. The ever increasing height of the high jump bar in track and field – and where the term "raising the bar" may originate from. Believability was developed about how high the bar could be raised but also what is achievable through experimentation and adaptation of jumping styles.

By far the best "See the Light" believability factor is when you experience it yourself. You can validate it, talk about it and teach it to others. It becomes yours - even if you were coached, mentored or supported - because you were the one that finally took the action necessary.

Get out of the same old, same old. The breakthroughs will come. Make "It can be done" the order of the day, in contrast to the old list of reasons why something couldn't be done. Soon you will be the expert in your support group, helping others and giving back.

Being on the breakthrough side of things is stirring. You stir people now. You stimulate them because *you* are stimulating. And it all starts with a new direction out of the same old routine. Then maintaining commitment and exposure to your support network until success is attained.

Now, how do you stay pumped and stay vibrant outside of you old routine, your old world? Well, you get to choose. Being vibrant is about exuding positive energy, activity, enthusiasm, liveliness. It is a vital key to success. It is about awareness of the vibrant, energetic, positive you that has had a taste of what is attainable.

MENTAL MUSCLE

Wherever you go, no matter what the weather,
always bring your own sunshine.

—Anthony J. D'Angelo

I am asked all of the time how I keep my energy level up and maintain a positive outlook. The answer is I don't. I have my dead times, energy wise, and I can lapse into the negative side of things, just like we all can. Everything is cyclical. However I am proud of the fact that I have had enough experience on both sides of the fence – success/growth and failure/setbacks. With the support of my network, I choose to always come back to the high energy, vibrant, positive side – the breakthrough side – as fast as possible. It is what gets me pumped up and what changes my state for the better every time.

I believe it takes three things to pull oneself out of the negative and into the positive at will.

1) Mental Muscle: Look in the mirror. You are fully responsible for your actions and mood. You choose your energy level and you choose your attitude. Each day is all made up anyway, like an acting part without a script. There is no way to know all that will happen and everyone you will come in contact with, or what will be said. You have creative control over your part of the script. I recommend you choose energetic, enthused, positive and vibrant. Make each day outstanding.

"Be happy while you're living, for you're a long time dead."

—*Scottish Proverb*

2) A Support Network: I have my Success Partner, Todd, and my Inner Circle Mastermind group to kick me in the behind and keep me accountable. They prevent me from falling to the pessimistic side of the diagram. You too have people in your support network more than willing to keep you on the right path. They will do more to create a great attitude toward yourself and toward any challenge you may be facing than anything else. Use them.

"A great attitude does much more than turn on the lights in our worlds; it seems to magically connect us to all sorts of serendipitous opportunities that were somehow absent before the change."

—**Earl Nightingale**

3) Action: Action trumps almost anything. In my experience, any person who is stuck, drifting to the negative, or is not having successes, is not taking sufficient action. Their commitment and discipline levels may be down. But basically, they just need to do as the Nike commercials say, "Just Do It".

"We need to practice acting in spite of fear, in spite of doubt, in spite of worry, in spite of uncertainty, in spite of inconvenience, in spite of discomfort, and even to practice acting when we're not in the mood to act."

—**T. Harv Eker, Author of #1 NY Times Bestseller**
Secrets of the Millionaire Mind

HOW'S IT GOING TODAY?

I start off almost every greeting, every phone call, every email and every conversation with, "How's it going today?" It is even on my voicemail. I like to say it first, with lots of positive energy. It changes my mood, my energy level – even when typing an email. I like to believe that it changes the other person's mood and energy level as well. Maybe there will be extra interest or better participation in a meeting or conversation, for both parties. It may even initiate more conversation. Who knows?

 DANNY DIAMOND SUCCESS TIP:

Have a greeting for people and greet them with high positive energy before they have a chance to greet you.

What if I get asked how I am?

I always say the same thing. "I am ALWAYS good!" With the emphasis on ALWAYS.

"If you don't think every day is a good day, just try missing one."

—Cavett Robert

Am I always good? Probably not. Okay, No! But I might as well be *good* while I am talking to someone because not being good isn't going to help with anything. I tell anyone that questions my *always good* statement that "there is no use feeling bad because the day is going to happen anyway." And I believe that. Why not live the day at the highest positive energy level you can muster? If you have to be out and about, why not participate at 100%? You can always feel bad later, on your own time.

Summary: Use the great "I believe in" and the "I want to have, experience and contribute" lists you created. Use your mental muscle and your support network. Take action followed by more action, followed by more action.

You will then stay on the breakthrough side of things. Your new diagram will look like the one below – where the whole quitting loop has been eliminated. Once it does, I recommend a trip back to Chapter 3, Your Comfort Zone, because when someone starts to achieve outside the Same Old, Same Old, it becomes easier to set new and higher goals – way outside their old comfort zone. Momentum becomes exponential instead of incremental.

Congratulations on the new vibrant you and welcome to your new world where Same Old, Same Old does not exist.

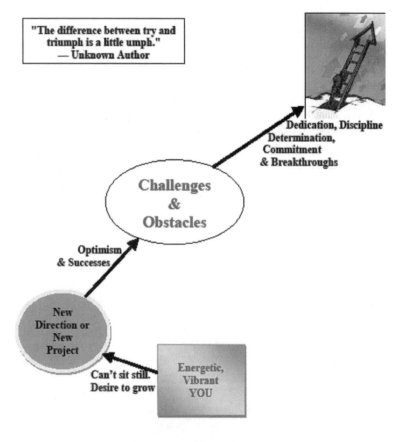

CHAPTER 6:

– High Flying to Giving Up and Everywhere In-between –

You are the person who has to decide;
Whether you'll do it or toss it aside.
You are the person who makes up your mind.
Whether you'll lead or will linger behind.
Whether you'll try for the goal that's afar.
Or just be contented to stay where you are.

– Unknown

THE "HIGH-FLYER"

My best marathon ever.

In pretty good shape, I was standing at the starting line area of the 2002 Calgary Marathon ready to take a crack at a completion time of under 4 hours, something I had not accomplished for awhile. It was July but the forecast was for a cool morning. Hot would be later in the day. I located the 4 hour pace bunny, my back up, with his sign held high and a group starting to gather under it. My intent was to run under 4 hours. If I struggled, the plan was to grab onto the 4 hour pace group to ensure that I reached my goal for the day.

As always, I had great support from my family who were all at the start line. I expected to see them along the course as well.

After speeches and announcements that none of us at the "back of the pack" could hear anyway, the gun sounded to start the race. The crowd of runners shuffled slowly through the narrow street that led to the start line. After several minutes, I finally crossed the timing sensor mats, heard the familiar beep from the timing chip on my running shoe being recognized, and started the timer on my watch.

There was lots of jockeying for position in the early going then we ran through the Zoo and over to Little Italy. In no time at all, it seemed, I was saying hi to Connie and the kids at the 10 kilometre marker on Memorial Drive. I was feeling pretty good. A bit warmer than expected but, hey, this was the Calgary Marathon and it was July. "I have broken 4 hours on a much hotter day", **I told myself**. But still..."**did I drink enough water early** on?" The mind chatter had started.

What you focus on expands!

It happened at the 16 kilometre mark. Out of nowhere goose bumps appeared on my arms. A few strides later I got a stitch in my side and my pace dropped off. I couldn't believe it - dehydration. "But I drank lots of water", I told myself. Forced to walk, I needed to regroup. Physically I just had to rehydrate as I went through the aid stations. A slow process that provides ample time for the mind to bring extra focus and negativity to the frustration of not attaining a goal or perhaps not even finishing the race.

As I walked, other runners streamed by including the 4 hour pace bunny group, soon followed by the 4:15 pace bunny group, then the 4:30 group sometime after that. Now I was talking out loud to myself. I blamed the course, the weather, the water and even the other runners. I was a mental mess and in full "oh woe is me" mode.

About the 20 kilometre mark where the course leaves the main road for the narrow pathways along the Bow River, the stream of runners going by stopped momentarily. The only sounds were my footsteps, my murmurs of bitching and feeling sorry for myself and...a shuffle step of some kind. I didn't bother to look back. Why would I? It was just another runner going to go past me and remind me again of what a disaster the day had turned out to be.

As the female runner with the shuffle step went by, about 5 meters to my left, I noticed that she had signs on her front and back. I looked a little closer and it said "blind runner". Now most people, and certainly me on a normal day, would have been amazed that a blind runner was even in the race, let alone that she was manoeuvring her way through the course without a partner or assistant. But it wasn't a normal day for me. As I sulked along I whispered to myself, "On top of everything else now even blind runners are passing me."

A few minutes later I left the main road for the trail heading toward the river where there is a favourite aid station of mine. The race organizers always had a calypso style drum band there. Plus there was a real bathroom (as opposed to outhouses at most other aid stations). The band was taking a break. Of course they were. Even though it was me, Danny Diamond, at the aid station, they had decided to take a break. As I went into the bathroom I remember thinking that if I had been able to keep my planned pace, I bet I would have come through this aid station when the band was playing. Oh woe is me.

I left the bathroom and went to grab water off the aid station table. I realized that something was wrong. The concern by the volunteers centered on the blind girl who had passed me just before the aid station. Apparently, she was confused when trying to leave the aid station and the volunteers were worried about her running alongside the river by herself. They discussed having a volunteer catch up to her while a volunteer at the next aid station headed this way. The plan was to meet about halfway and do the exchange of acting as her guide. Without even thinking, or remembering that I was supposed to be dehydrated, disappointed and miserable, I heard myself blurt out, "I'll go with her if that helps." The volunteers accepted my offer right away. It was only after they had thanked me that I clarified my previous statement with, "If I can catch her."

Funny what a change of focus does to a person. "What you focus on expands". I forgot about myself and my problems for awhile and, instead, turned the anxiousness to 'catch her before she fell in the river' into the best running form and pace I had all day. I caught up to her in no time and the "real" marathon began.

I introduced myself as did she – we'll call her Wendy. After a few intervals – running for 5 minutes and walking for 1 minute – Wendy realized that I was sticking around. I didn't tell her that I was sent by the aid station volunteers to make sure she did not fall into the Bow River. Wendy did not want me to hang around and detailed a story of the Edmonton Marathon just a few weeks before.

Edmonton, Alberta was the actual marathon Wendy had trained for over the winter. Her mother insisted she run with friends of the family in the race, making Wendy uncomfortable and feeling under pressure to perform. On a horrendously hot day, where dehydration and heat stroke made more headlines and stories in the newspapers than those who completed the race, the male friend of Wendy's family could not continue after the half way point. Although not suffering from the heat herself, Wendy used the situation as an excuse to quit because it had not been the experience she had hoped for.

Wendy went home and immediately entered the Calgary Marathon.

The reason she did not want me hanging around was because she was worried that I might affect her completing the race in some way, much like she felt had happened in Edmonton. I assured her that I would remain in the back ground and was only there to support. In fact, I told her that no matter how my marathon day goes, I always finish and, therefore, she too would be finishing this race. That seemed to ease her mind and we shuffled along together. Quietly at first but anyone that knows me, knows that **I can't stay shut-up for long.** I was running with a marvel, a "no-fear" type of person, and I had a bazillion questions.

How did she see?

Wendy told me that if the sun was shining, as it was on this particular race day, she could see shadows about 4 or 5 metres in front of her to the side and, if the road had an edge or curb, she could use that as a guide.

How long had she been blind? Since birth.

Had she trained for the marathon?

Yes, at an indoor track. The lighting was such that she could use the inside rail of the track as her guide. She built up to 20 miles as her longest run on the track.

Why a marathon?

Wendy told me that a marathon was such a significant milestone for most runners that it had been a goal of hers for quite some time.

What other sports had she done?

She made the school swim team but, with much disappointment in her voice, was never allowed to swim at a meet. I said, "Swimming blind…how tough is that?" Her reply was simple and with a smile – "you hit the lane dividers a lot".

What else?

Wendy said, "the school track club." What??? Yes. She said her dad dropped her off in the early morning hours before school started and she trained with the track club. School safety policies prevented her from being able to complete in a meet.

What else?

Wendy was attending the Red Deer College; in Red Deer, Alberta. She tried out and made the cross-country team. Before I could ask, her face lit up with a smile. She had finally got to compete in a race, the very first meet of the cross country season, with a guide running with her. "What was it like running through the trees?" I asked. "Pretty scratchy", was her reply, again with a smile.

Who was down from Edmonton (approximately a 3 hour drive) to watch her on this incredibly important marathon day?

She had travelled with her aunt who would meet her at the finish line.

Where are your mom and dad?

They didn't come down and neither did her sister. Wendy shared with me that her dad had never seen her run, at least not that she knew of. She explained the reasons but suffice it to say; she really, really wanted her dad to see her run someday. I hope he has.

By the time we were getting close to the 30 kilometre mark, the sun was beating down in all its glory. Wendy's pace had slowed down considerably. I started doing calculations in my head. At the current pace, we would finish after the course was officially closed. At the next aid station, out of Wendy's ear shot, I explained the situation to a few of the volunteers and asked them if they could radio on ahead to the finish line with the request that they please leave the finish line up for Wendy and, if at all possible, have a race photographer on-hand to take a picture so that Wendy would have an official finish line photo. They said they would do what they could.

Wendy did a great job on kilometres 31 and 32. One step past the 32 kilometre mark (20 miles), we had a big celebration. Alongside the Bow River, arms in the air and shouting and whistling. The recreational joggers and cyclists going by gave us questioning looks wondering what these two people, one wearing "Blind Runner" signs, were so happy about.

Wendy, during her training, had never gone further than 20 miles, or 32 kilometres. Every step past the 32 kilometre mark was now a personal distance record for her. It was very exciting.

At kilometre 33 we had a similar celebration and the great volunteers at the aid station there, cheered with us even though they did not know why we were celebrating. I again asked the volunteers to radio on ahead to the finish line to keep it intact and have a photographer for Wendy, if possible.

The very enlightening conversation continued (it was definitely enlightening to me) and we were soon celebrating at kilometres 34 and 35 as she continued to set personal bests. For the first time Wendy mentioned that her legs were stiffening and asked "how much further?" I reminded her that quitting was not an option.

Each of Kilometres 36, 37, 38 and 39 seemed to take forever to complete. Lots of rests and we were now walking pretty much 100% of the time. Despite what had to be pain with each step for her, she never complained – it wasn't her style. The celebrations at each kilometre marker continued and the volunteers kept contacting the finish line as per my requests.

Normally my family would have met me at several locations on the marathon course during the race. I had not seen them since kilometre 10 and I assumed that I was so far behind my usual pace they had no idea where I was or why. I have carried a cell phone with me in every race since then.

Shortly after leaving the last official aid station at Kilometre 39, we met up with The Beautiful and Vivacious Mrs. Connie Lyon. Even though the volunteers could not confirm if I was still on the course, Connie was confident I was and she had walked in from the finish line to see if I might need some support to finish. I introduced Connie to Wendy, highlighting the accomplishment and what an inspiration she was. Connie relayed the information by cell phone to the rest of the family waiting at the finish line – our three kids, Tommy 9, Davey 7, Maggie 5; Connie's sister Kathy and Kathy's two daughters, Breanne 11 and Katie 9.

The last couple of kilometres were amongst the trees along the river and the shade was very much appreciated. The marathon course was such that when you broke out of the trees to head to the finish line at Fort Calgary, there was about 150 meters on a regular city street – which meant back into the blazing sun. But this time "in the blazing sun" **meant** with the end in sight or, for Wendy, knowledge that the finish line was just ahead.

As Wendy, Connie and I came out of the trees, all 5 kids ran for us. They could have cared less about me. They wanted to see Wendy. "Are you really blind?" "How come you can see some stuff if you are really blind?" "Can you see me when I jump in front of you?" (and a few of them took turns jumping in front of her) "Can you see me when I am over to the side like this?" "Can you watch TV?" "How do you get your homework done?" "Do you go to school?" "Can you drive a car?"

Progressing towards the finish line as a group, I asked the kids to stop asking questions and mind their manners. Wendy insisted it was okay. She said that kids were the best to talk with about her blindness because they were the most open and honest – and she tried to answer every question the kids were firing at her.

I was pleased to see that the race organizers and volunteers had left the finish line intact and there was indeed a photographer on hand. Only a hand full of people were left at the finish line to witness what was, in my opinion, one of the most outstanding marathon finishes I have ever been a part of.

As we got closer to the finish line, the kids branched off back to the spectator area. I stopped Wendy with about 15 meters to go. I explained to her that the official finish line was still standing, and that when she felt the soft cushion of the timing system mats under her feet, she needed to raise both arms high in the air. I told her she would be finishing on her own and that in the tradition of all marathoners, it was important that she run, not walk, across the finish line. Wendy completed the race perfectly and extended her arms at exactly the right time for the photographer. She continued forward to receive her medal and then into the waiting arms of her ecstatic and very emotional Aunt.

Excellent stuff.

Wendy was so proud of her finisher's medal. I told her that when she got home, she needed to walk right up to her dad, put the medal around his neck and give him a big kiss, because he had missed something very special. I wonder if she followed through on that. I hope so.

On the drive home, my son Tommy announced that he was not just going to be able to tell everyone that his dad finished last in the Calgary Marathon. Instead, he would be able to tell them that his dad finished dead last. But you know, I may have been dead last, but it was the best finish I have ever had in *any* race. What an inspiration Wendy was that day - and I am sure she still inspires those around her. It was my best marathon ever.

When someone tells me that they have it too tough and they "can't" do something, or I find myself questioning my ability to do something, I think back to the inspiration Wendy provided and the guts and determination she exemplified.

Wendy is a "High Flyer" in my books.

As Bob Proctor mentions frequently: "Go to the edge, jump off, and develop wings on the way down". As far as I can tell, Wendy has done exactly that for all of her young life.

THE "TURN-AROUND ARTIST"

The last 10 years of my 20 plus years in Telecommunications was spent outside of Canada - in the U.S., Puerto Rico, and Guam. The final four years were in Thailand where our two youngest, Davey and Maggie, were born. We decided it was time to do something else.

In the fall of 1995, while still living in Bangkok, Connie and I made the decision to open a Mail Boxes Etc. Franchise in our home city of Lethbridge, Alberta.

We left Thailand in March, 1996 and opened our store in June, 1996.

My sister Penny agreed to manage the store for the first year and my nieces Lisa and Jaclyn hired on as sales associates. They would run the store and Connie and I planned to take one more Telecom assignment in Brazil or Mexico. As it turned out, after long lease negotiations for the premises and my commitment to Penny to work the business with her for 2 months after opening – we were getting pretty settled. When a house became available close to Connie's father's house on the same park, we made the decision to stay.

Led by Connie's extraordinary marketing abilities, and the world class customer service of Penny, Lisa and Jaclyn, we had much success right from the get-go, winning awards in our very first year.

We were working on plans to own and operate more stores when we were presented with the opportunity to purchase the Mail Boxes Etc. Area Franchise rights for the Provinces of Alberta and Saskatchewan.

Assisting others to get into business and then supporting them, was intriguing. Connie's sister Kathy partnered with us in the venture and the deal was successfully completed in September, 1998.

Thus began my real education on the subject of business ownership and "High Flyers" to "Give-ups" and everywhere in between.

My naivety that all Franchisees followed the Franchise system and ran their business like we did became both a detriment and a blessing. A detriment because I was caught off guard and had to rethink growth strategies for the Area. I also had to be more accepting and open minded about each Franchisee's personality and strengths as well as their needs, hopes and desires for their business. It was a blessing for the exact same reasons. The Franchisees continue to give me an education on business every day.

In 1998, Andrew Kang had been the owner of his Mail Boxes Etc. for over 4 years. Unbeknownst to me, he was at the point of shutting his doors and walking away from his business about the same time we were taking over as Area Franchisees. I found this out in the first quarter of 1999 when Andrew and I met for a business performance review. From franchise meetings the previous 2 years, I had pegged Andrew as being fairly negative about the business and expected the performance review to have challenges. However, I was greeted with perhaps the best set of books and numbers I have ever seen from a Franchisee, in addition to a list of ideas on how he might turn things around. He was not talking like the old Andrew.

What had changed?

Andrew had recently failed an audit by Head Office. He didn't fail because he had been misreporting or cheating. He failed because he couldn't produce required invoices and other support documentation, due to his "non-existent" filing system. At the same time Revenue Canada was applying pressure for proper reporting and filing.

Andrew finally asked for help. His network came through, assisting in setting up a proper filing system and set of books to analyze the business. It was these items coupled with Andrew's new and refreshing approach towards business that made our review together much better than I ever would have expected.

In his own words, Andrew says,

"The option of walking away from the business was one that I almost took. *The feeling at that time was anger, frustration, trapped, loss, in debt and that everything "sucks". Does the idea of "cut my losses" really work? Is the landlord going to cease rent payments? Are Revenue Canada and utility companies going to forego collections? Does the business really stop just because I walked away?*

What stops for sure is the revenue stream. Money aside, how would I feel bumping into one of my hundreds of customers? More importantly, how would I be able to look at my daughter? If one contemplates a sudden business exit, let it be planned. It's very hard to hide.

Ignoring or closing my eyes to what I do not like costs. I am not a bookkeeper but insisted on doing the books myself to save costs. During the challenging times, I disliked accounting tasks even more as I did not want to know about the business losses. The spiralling downward effect finally resulted in Revenue Canada shutting down my banking. Therefore, it was not self-revelation that got me to bring my accounting up to date.

What did I do to turn things around? Was there a defining moment? Perhaps feeling my back against the wall, the only way possible was forward. **Perhaps, I realized that constant complaining and blaming did not help pay the bills and they certainly did not deter the collection phone calls.**

Once I had the accounting system in front of me, I cringed when I saw how much NSF penalties had contributed to my losses. The penalties were more than enough to hire a part time bookkeeper and I would have much less stress.

There was no grand plan to get out of the hole. There were small steps. The new accounting system revealed the profitable areas. Redirecting my focus and efforts to these areas resulted in increased sales and profits. This momentum then rubbed off on other profit centres.

The business was sold years later in 2007. During that time, my store consistently appeared on Page 1 of the Franchise Ranking Report and was a top performer in Copy sales. It progressively established itself to be a "resource" store for other franchisees. There were even achievement awards displayed on the wall. With the rather pleasant turn of events, there was more profitable work, but at the same time, I had more free time to explore and enjoy other interests, one of them being Tea.

I exited not by throwing away the key but with lots of goodwill behind me. I was able to shake the hands of my customers and thank them. Again, more importantly, I was able to enjoy the start of another new journey with my daughter.

*Certainly, there were lessons learned. Being organized and keeping an up to date accounting system is crucial. **Having a networking system not so much for blaming and venting but for brainstorming and sharing is invaluable.** Making changes in small forward moving increments builds momentum. In other words, do not expect to change long time habits overnight. Now, looking back to 1999 and with a bit of tea lifestyle philosophy...get connected with the moment and yourself."*

Andrew is now the proud owner of his latest business venture, Elixir Fine Tea in Calgary, Alberta (*www.elixirfinetea.com*).

Andrew shared three important thoughts that day in 1999 that I have used continuously since then, as if my own.

1. He told me that once he had a proper set of books to analyze, he finally knew "***how money left the building***". Money came into the business over the counter and was punched into his cash register. But the *outgoing* flow of money for costs of goods and fixed expenses had never been in control. For the first time in his business life he realized how much his photocopiers were costing him, how much he was spending on marketing and

payroll, and how much profit margin he was achieving in the various profit centers.

2. Andrew told me that when he analyzed his numbers for what was, essentially, the very first time, he "**became a businessman that day**", with a new attitude.

3. Andrew said that one of his biggest successes was *finally* **asking for help**. Instead of trying to do it all himself or keep his problems hidden from as many people as possible, there was a relief in asking others for help. Andrew had *exposed* himself and his network was there for him (as they always are for everyone).

In any struggling store or struggling Franchisee scenario that has developed since then, I have shared Andrew's story. In virtually every case where the Franchisee took the time to analyze "how the money leaves the building", took the time to ask for help from their network, and then took action, they have either turned their business around completely and kept the store, or added enough value to the business in order to sell it at a much higher price than they would have otherwise.

DANNY DIAMOND SUCCESS TIP:

This "how money leaves the building" analysis works just as well for personal finances as it does for business finances.

If you ever feel you are struggling with cash flow personally, do a financial analysis to discover exactly "how money leaves the building". Then do what Andrew did - use your network to work on solutions for making the 180 degree turn.

As for Andrew, 2 years later he was the top store in sales in our Area and became a leader. I remember the first time Andrew stood up at a meeting to shut down a complaining Franchisee. Another long time Franchisee hit me in the arm, pointed at Andrew and asked "who's the new guy"? A very good question because Andrew was 180 degrees from where he had been. What had seemed impossible to him was now possible.

> *I'm a great believer in luck, and I find the*
> *harder I work, the more luck I have.*
>
> —Thomas Jefferson

Andrew also became a mentor to other store owners. In one example, he agreed to meet with a struggling Franchisee in a very similar negative cycle to the one Andrew had been in. When I called later to see how it went, Andrew told me that they did not meet. He had made the call and set it up but then his last question to the other franchisee was "are you ready to look in the mirror?" When the answer came back "No", Andrew told the other Franchisee that he could not help him and to try would be a waste of time. He was right.

 DANNY DIAMOND SUCCESS TIP:

You can't help someone who won't take responsibility for where they are, good or bad. You can't help someone who won't help themselves, whether it be in business, in their work, or in their personal lives. Anyone not willing to take responsibility for their successes and failures, not willing to look in the mirror, is blocking their own way on the path to success.

A consultant once shared with me that in his 20 years of experience working with franchise systems and owners, 25% of Franchisees were going to be hugely successful, 50% ranged everywhere from low to moderate to good success, and 25% were destined to struggle more than they ever needed to, sometimes failing completely. He went on to state that the difference in performance, top to bottom, had less to do with intellect, knowledge, ability, location, and business type than it had to do with attitude, willingness to do whatever it takes, following the proven systems. I agree.

I would like to take it one step further in that I believe the percentages and differences in performances relate to work, career and to one's personal life as well.

Following are my definitions of the categories I believe people fall into.

Please note that we all have some of each category in us and we all have the capability to move to another category any time we wish.

THE "GIVE-UPS"

"Hard work spotlights the character of people: some turn up their sleeves, some turn up their noses, and some don't turn up at all."

—Sam Ewing

"Give-Ups" say they want success but do not do the work necessary or are not willing to suffer any discomfort in overcoming problems or obstacles. People in this category are looking for the "magic pill" that will fix everything (like winning the lottery). They like to hear about and record new ideas but do not take action or carry through to any degree. This group is at the highest level of blaming others for their lack of success and complaining about their plight.

"Give-Ups" are forever having trouble getting their 'Success' airplane up to speed and off the ground. They tend not to utilize mentors and advisors who have had the success they say they want. Instead, "Give-Ups" attract people on board who generally agree that taking off is too difficult and that getting to their destination goal probably isn't worth the effort.

"So many fail because they don't get started; they don't go. They don't overcome inertia. They don't begin."

—W. Clement Stone

The most important trait of any category, "**Ultimate Customer Commitment**", is the lowest in the "Give-Up" group. When focus has become about "me and my problems", as it has with the "Give-Ups", it is very difficult to have ultimate customer commitment to anyone that comes in contact with them.

DANNY DIAMOND SUCCESS TIP:

The "Ultimate Customer Commitment" is a great tool to use when deciding whether you would like, relationship wise, to move closer to a person or further away from a person – as in the exercise you did in Chapter 1.

Customers of businesses make this determination all of the time. They judge the ability and commitment of the business to Get, Keep and Satisfy the person who has the most value to the business success – the customer – and decide whether they will move closer or move further away.

I believe from a personal aspect, making this same determination with everyone in your network – their ability and commitment to get, keep and satisfy you as a member of their network – has great value in determining whether you should move closer or move further away from a person.

THE "RESISTORS"

"Resistors" can sometimes have a lot of success - by their standards. Typically though, this group usually works much harder than they have to, and struggles to gain any kind of sustained momentum.

"Resistors" are sceptical of all existing systems and are resistant to any changes. They believe the way they do things, is best. They do not "expose" themselves for success and utilization of Peers–Mentors–Advisors is centered on other "Resistors" or no one at all, as they tend to want to fight battles alone. They do have better knowledge of their strengths but stubbornly resist adapting or stretching away from those strengths, even if it means continuing to struggle or getting in their own way of personal, professional or business success.

This is the group that if you told them that turning the key to the right would open 'the door' they would turn it to the left to see if you were right. "Resistors" choose not to implement new ideas or act on what could be great opportunities unless it fits into their program. There is more vision and planning of what they want for their life, their career, their business than with the "Give-Ups". This group is very opinionated and they have an agenda.

This "Resistors" group will taxi out in their airplane but will question the air traffic control tower on the runway being used and the direction designated for take-off. They will go with a bare minimum crew feeling that less means less headaches. "Resistors" prefer to do the piloting themselves. They are extremely resistant to having passengers, except on their terms, and therefore limit their customer base and growth.

I believe "Resistors" better understand the importance of the customer than the "Give-Ups" but their "**Ultimate Customer Commitment**", in all aspects of their lives, is still very low. "**Ultimate Customer Commitment**" will always be low in individuals whose focus is on "me and my problems" and not on getting, keeping and satisfying customers or people in their network.

 DANNY DIAMOND SUCCESS TIP:

The way to determine your own "Ultimate Customer Commitment" is easy.

And, again, the word *customer* does not just mean a customer of your business or where you work. Customer means anyone personally or professionally who is in your network or could be in your network.

If you like to complain about how things are and blame others for mistakes that are affecting your life, you are probably focussed on "me and my problems". We all do this at times so we all have a certain level of "me and my problems".

How high is your "me and my problems" level?

The rule is this: the higher the level of "me and my problems" focus you have, the lower the level of your "Ultimate Customer Commitment". In other words, the more you blame others for your problems, the less likely you will be able to get, keep and satisfy customers - personally, professionally and in business.

Because of their "Belief Management", their inability to look in the mirror and take responsibility for their situation, anyone spending additional time trying to support and help "Give-Ups" and "Resistors" are wasting their time and are probably having a lot of energy sucked out of them. Typically, "Resistors" have to hit bottom before any change will occur.

THE "COMFORT ZONE DWELLERS"

We all fit into this category at one time or another, no matter what level of success we have achieved. Health, tiredness, age, change of values, change of desires, etc., are all factors. In my experience, for highly successful people and high achievers, any time spent as a "Comfort Zone Dweller" is only temporary.

What I mean by "Comfort Zone Dwellers" is the category of people who do all that is necessary to get to a comfortable level of success and then won't leave. More conservative than risk adverse, their business comfort zone may be break even, or making a certain level of income from the business. In their personal lives their comfort zone may be in covering the bills, having a certain level of income coming in, attaining a certain amount of savings, or having certain possessions that make them feel comfortable. One could argue that a positive about "Comfort Zone Dwellers" is their dependability and predictability.

For vision and planning, they don't shoot for the stars but they do like to achieve within their level of comfort. "Comfort Zone Dwellers" may even take a swing at expanding their comfort zone from time to time. Reasons may be life changes, believability factor (have seen peer's successes), and support from others.

"Comfort Zone Dwellers" typically recognize that in many aspects they are in their own way on their road to success. But they don't complain about it as much as the previous two groups and they will get out of their way in their good time and on their terms. Their ability to detail their strengths and weaknesses (the "exposing" so others can help), is not seen as a necessity.

This group will typically take-off in their success airplane, but will not want to fly too high. They too don't want the headaches of a lot of staff but will at least have some to help service the comfortable level of customers they have attracted. Preferring to pilot their 'Success' airplane themselves, they like shorter flights so that there is time to reassess and regroup - feel more comfortable and safe – more often.

"**Ultimate Customer Commitment**" for "Comfort Zone Dwellers", is only as strong as what will fit into their level of comfort. Since they focus less on "me and my problems" they naturally attract more customers, a bigger network. "Comfort Zone Dwellers" have huge potential to fly high in their success airplane if they want.

THE "TURN-AROUND ARTISTS"

This group may be my favourite. Highly successful people are motivating because of all of their ongoing energy and accomplishments. "Turn-Around Artists" like Andrew's story above, are inspirational because of what they have to overcome within themselves to reverse the direction they were going. Anyone in any of the categories can become a "Turn-Around Artist" and that is exciting to me because this group increases the "success is attainable" believability factor for everyone!

To set things in motion, a "Turn-Around Artist" usually capitalizes on hitting rock bottom, being given ultimatums, or realizing what the effect of where they are going will have on people close to them. This combines with a willingness to stay and fight instead of giving up.

Using the 'Success' airplane metaphor again, this group has been trying to take off for a long time without having a clear flight plan or destination and usually have been blaming everyone else for everything that has gone wrong to date. They attract staff but go through a lot of them and they do the same with customers who get tired of the lack of direction and image. Luckily, somewhere along the line, this person catches a glimpse of themselves in the mirror and realizes they have the pilot's uniform on and are indeed the one responsible. And if they announce the news that they are responsible, as in "expose" themselves, they suddenly get a lot more help from the tower, other pilots, the staff and customers.

For "Turn-Around Artists":

- **Vision** and **Planning** moves to a high level because many of the limitations that were holding them back are being shattered as they recognize the potential.

- They have taken the look in the mirror, stopped blaming and complaining for the most part, and are ready to take full responsibility for their success or failure.

- **Adaptability** to change was low while they were trudging along blaming everyone and everything. Now, the "Turn-Around Artist" is willing to look at all **Opportunities** as their whole world vision has expanded.

- Utilization of **Peers–Mentors–Advisors** is now accepted and "exposing themselves for success" is now the norm.

- The "**Ultimate Customer Commitment**" has jumped from low to high. "Me and my problems" is exchanged for "if it is going to be, it is up to me". Focus on their customers and their network has become a priority. The once grounded or stalled success airplane is now taking off and the "Turn around Artist" is adding people to help it fly high.

THE "CAN-DOERS"

I believe everyone has the talent to achieve much more than they presently do but said talent is sometimes overridden by their "Give-Up", "Resistor", or "Comfort Zone" tendencies. In this Chapter, the "Can-Doers" are the ones that are "doing it" and are hungry for more.

This group may have come from any of the other categories previously discussed. These are the top 25% people mentioned in the consultant's workshop. They typically started with clear vision, goals and planning. These are action takers – "Doers". They have complaints and concerns but usually structure them in ways to work towards finding solutions. They have leadership qualities. They know that support from others, supporting others and being a team player are important. They work through any scepticism and then take action. "Can-Doers" possess lots of energy and can motivate others to attain more success.

Their 'Success' plane has well trained staff. The customers they attract refer other customers to them.

"Can-Doer's" know they are the pilot yet have ensured that others are trained to fly the plane. When in the air, they are comfortable at a high altitude and don't mind if they have to climb higher in order to make the trip better or faster.

This group, the "Can-Doers", have the following characteristics:

- **Vision** and **Planning** is at a high level. If you asked them for a business plan they would have it. If working for someone else they could show the vision and plan for the company and for their department. In their personal lives, they know what they want and where they are going.

- **Honesty With Themselves** - This group looks in the mirror regularly, naturally expecting the responsibility of success or failure to rest on their shoulders. Their ability to detail strengths and weaknesses and expose themselves so that others can help is a priority.

- **Adaptability** and the willingness to change are high. **Opportunities** abound.

- "Can-Doers" know that **Peers–Mentors–Advisors** are a necessity and they are typically and most times natural mentors and advisors themselves. They want to be around other successful people and want to hear every best idea or best practice so that they can utilize it themselves.

- Their "Belief Management" is extremely high and they work hard to make sure they don't stand in their own way on the road to success.

- "**Ultimate Customer Commitment**" is also extremely high. They truly get that the reason to get up in the morning is to get, keep and satisfy customers.

THE "HIGH FLYERS"

This is the group most dream about being in. In small business, this is the group that is so eloquently described in the books "The E-Myth" and "The E-Myth Revisited" by Michael Gerber. This group knows that to attain true and total success, they have to be the leader and visionary and overseer of their business or life and can no longer be the one on the front lines as the main "Doer".

In my experience, the "High Flyers" would have been successful at anything they tried in any business type or model that came on their radar screen. They understand that the more their business can run without their day to day involvement, the more value it has. And they realize that the more personal, financial and time freedom they can accomplish, the more they can give back in money and time to help others grow and enjoy more successes.

"High Flyers" are always looking for *bigger and better* and through their success and experience become great mentors and solution finders. They inspire, excite and motivate.

Concerning their success plane, "High Flyers" probably helped build or improve the airport and helped shape and make better air controller operations. They recognize, develop and utilize teams as much as possible. Their goal is to fly higher than ever before while helping everyone else to fly higher than ever before.

The "High-Flyers", have the following characteristics:

- **Vision** and **Planning** is of the highest priority and where all success originates.

- **Honesty With Themselves** – they have detailed their strengths and weaknesses and exposed themselves so many times that, with little effort, everyone around them recognizes their desire to help and be helped.

- **Adaptability** and capitalizing on **Opportunities** are the major factors of their success. No stone is left unturned.

- They utilize **Peers–Mentors–Advisors** and are mentors and advisors themselves. They understand that it is a team effort – whether it is personal or business – and the team takes priority over the individual.

*"If you are going to play the game at a high level,
you need to study or mentor with someone who
plays the game at a high level."*

- **Bob Proctor, Personal Development Guru,
Author and star of the movie "The Secret".**

- "Belief Management" is extremely high. They not only stay out of their own success path they clear the road for so many other people. The "High-Flyer" is constantly raising the bar, which carries everyone else to a much higher level too.

- They wrote the book on get, keep and satisfy customers and they use "**Ultimate Customer Commitment**" to maximize their investment and their legacy – both personally and in business.

So, which one are you? A "Give-Up", a "Resistor", a "Comfort Zone Dweller", a "Turn Around Artist", a "Can-Doer", or a "High Flyer"?

Perhaps you are a mixture of all 6 categories. Perhaps you are really strong in one but definitely have the traits of one or two others. Perhaps you have noticed that because you are strong in one category, it has been holding you back in another. Let's find out.

Remember that each category pertains to, or can relate to your business, professional or personal life separately. Perhaps you are a "High Flyer" in business but a "Resistor" or "Comfort Zone Dweller" in your personal life. Perhaps you are a "Can-Doer" in your personal life but are a "Give-Up" in your current career. And perhaps you are like many people that fit into the same category personally, as you do in your job, career or business.

EXERCISE 12:

1. Please complete the following for both your personal life and for your professional/business life.

After reviewing the descriptions of each person type as described above, and on a scale of 1-10, 10 meaning that "this category definitely describes me", please complete the following exercise by rating yourself for each category.

*Note: a template of these forms is available at www. thecolourofmyunderwearisblue.com

Category	Personal Life Scale of 1-10	Career/Professional/ Business Scale of 1-10
A "Give-up"		
A "Resistor"		
A "Comfort Zone Dweller"		
A "Turn Around Artist"		
A "Can-Doer"		
A "High Flyer"		

2. In the chart below, list the 3 highest scoring categories from the exercise above in both your personal life and in your career/professional/business life. In the adjacent columns, detail why you feel you are in this category; is it positive or negative for you to remain in this category. Also, if you wanted to move out of this category into another one, what would that category be and would you need to do or change in order to get there.

Top 3 Personal Categories:

Category	Why Do I Feel I am in this Category in my Personal Life?	Is it Positive or Negative for me to remain in this Category? Why?	If I wanted to move out of this Category into another one, what Category would I move to and what would I need to do or change to get there?
1)			
2)			
3)			

Top 3 Career/Professional/Business Categories:

Category	Why Do I Feel I am in this Category in my Career, Professional/ Business Life?	Is it Positive or Negative for me to remain in this Category? Why?	If I wanted to move out of this Category into another one, what Category would I move to and what would I need to do or change to get there?
1)			
2)			
3)			

Can you move categories? YES!!

Who controls where you are now, and where you end up?

You do. It is always the same. That never changes. Success is a choice.

DANNY DIAMOND SUCCESS TIP:

Whether YOU choose to be successful or unsuccessful.......it is your choice. Yes?

Whether YOU choose to be successful or unsuccessful, take full responsibility that you are the one responsible.

The Mindset Magnet - just as a magnet attracts, so does a person attract the same type of mindset in another person. Good or bad; successful or unsuccessful; Can do attitude or cannot. That is why "Give-up's" seem to like to hang out with other "Give-up's". It is who they attract.

DANNY DIAMOND SUCCESS TIP:

No matter what category you put yourself in above, if you would like to move to a different category, the fastest way is to change your mindset such that you start to attract those in the category you aspire to.

The fastest way to change your mindset it to make a conscious effort, take the actions necessary, to move away from those in your current category, and move closer to those in the category you aspire to.

Sit with these people at meetings. Ask them out for coffee or lunch. Ask them to mentor you. They are waiting, and have been waiting a long time in many cases, to help you make the impossible, possible.

CHAPTER 7:

– *Mind Your Business* –

"Far better it is to dare mighty things, to win glorious triumphs, even though chequered by failure, than to take rank with those poor spirits who neither enjoy much nor suffer much, because they live in the gray twilight that knows not victory nor defeat."

—Theodore Roosevelt

"Always bear in mind that your own resolution to succeed is more important than any other one thing."

—Abraham Lincoln

A very high percentage of people have a desire to be in their own business. I am of the philosophy that everyone, no matter what their age, job, position, career or personal situation, is really a business person and in business already - whether they own and operate a business or not.

My grandfather used to watch the 11 pm nightly news, go to bed, and be up at 4 am, so that he was down at the family business by 5 am. Once in a while, Jimmy and I were allowed to get up and go with my grandfather on a Saturday to "**help**" him open the business. Airway

Motors, the "Garage" as everyone called it, was a full-serve service station also offering bulk fuel, vehicle sales and repair, tire sales and service and fishing and hunting sporting goods.

On weekdays, my grandfather would return home for an early lunch with my grandmother and then have a power nap before heading back to the Garage for the afternoon. Most Saturdays, my grandfather would drive my grandmother into "town" (meaning Lethbridge, 30 miles away) and we would get to go. My grandmother shopped at Kresgees and Woolworths down town and then rode the bus out to Woolcos (she always said Woolco with an "s" on the end even though it didn't have one, which became a family joke). While she was shopping, Jimmy and I would be with our grandfather picking up parts and running errands for the Garage. A late lunch was always at the Legion where, as far as I was concerned, they had the best bacon omelette ever created. One or two more stops after lunch then we would meet my grandmother at the back of the Eatons department store downtown. Then home to Barons.

> *"There is less to fear from outside competition than from inside inefficiency, discourtesy and bad service."*
>
> - Anonymous

On one trip, a parts place did not have the part we required. Rather than my grandfather driving all over town to find it, the parts guy phoned around to several of his competitors. I was young but I found this amazing that a business would do the footwork for a customer with the full intent to send us to a *competitor*! What great customer service. It stuck with me. When we opened our Mail Boxes Etc. store in 1996, we put a policy in place that, if ever in a similar situation, we would try our utmost to do exactly for our customers what the parts guy did for my grandfather that day. It wows the socks off a customer when you are able to perform this service.

As a youngster, I thought this being in business thing was pretty good, especially since I didn't have to do any of the work. What I didn't know at the time was how much I was learning about commerce and customer service on main street, and how much owning my own business would attract me later in life.

Time spent with Mr. Peacock at the telephone office and Mr. Johnson at his TV/Radio repair shop, helped create my interest in telecommunications and electronics.

At the butcher shop, Mr. Kurtin would let me read comic books for free. I would tuck in out of sight along the wall by the comic stand, and spend hours there. Most importantly, I had the privilege to watch a cross-selling, up selling, customer service master, Mr. Kurtin, at work.

Slim's convenience store was the place to bring pop bottles we found in the ditches around town for the two cent deposit - which we immediately spent on candy. Jimmy and I also used Slim's store to buy cigarettes when we went through that period of experimenting with "smokes" starting when we were 9 and 10 or so. The scam was always the same. Jimmy would bum 25 cents off either my Dad or my grandfather at the Garage. Then I would bum 25 cents off the other. 50 cents was the price of a pack of cigarettes and Slim rarely questioned us on who they were for. We would then ride our bikes up to the baseball diamond and puff away. When we eventually got caught, Dad made us sit at the kitchen table and inhale every drag for two cigarettes. Having never inhaled before, I was sick and the urge to ever smoke again was gone forever.

My Mother was a huge bookkeeping influence. She showed me how to set up a set of books, post receivables and payables, send out statements and how to balance the daily cash after closing. Although unaware at the time, these were my first lessons in "how money leaves the building".

My grandfather helped me start-up a lawn mowing service, my first experience of being self-employed, when I was 10.

Now there was a high margin business. I used my grandfather's mower and gas, and I kept all of the profits. He was even one of my paying customers for his lawn. Aren't grandfathers great?

I mowed lawns in town for years and it was always a bone of contention with my Dad that I would willingly mow other people's lawns, yet I whined and bellyached about mowing our lawn at home (just like my brothers did).

THE STORE

Roy and Dorothy Dayman owned Dayman's General Store in Barons. I was hanging around outside the store one day when I was about 11 and Roy put me to work cleaning out the back room, where all of the empty boxes were stored. The best part about it was that I got to burn all of the boxes he did not want or need. Roy paid me $1 an hour for a couple of hours work but I would have done it for free to get the chance to burn the boxes. I filled the burning barrel, which was out by the back alley away from any buildings, stacked most of the rest of the boxes all around the barrel and kept some boxes to the side so I could keep stoking the fire (and prolong the event for as long as possible). I then set it on fire. Roy decided that he had waited too long to clean the back room - I think meaning that there was too many boxes and the fire got too big. So he asked me if I could give him one afternoon a week after school to keep the back room clean. Of course I said yes if for nothing else than I was going to get to light a fire once a week, with an adult's permission.

Soon after my first ever weekly work schedule got going, Roy gave me more hours. He and Dorothy taught me how to clean and stock shelves; how to change out the magazines and send the non-sellers back; and how to change out the produce. I did a lot of deliveries as well, especially to Mr. Duncan who was pretty much house bound after years in the coal mines. Mr. Duncan bought a lot of Buckley's Mixture to help the coughing and I would try to stay as long as possible because his stories were great.

Eventually Roy let me work on the front counter and taught me how to cut cheese and bacon; how to wrap meats and cheese in paper (and the art of tying and snapping off the string that we put on all wrapped goods); and how to utilize those extra boxes in the back to pack people's groceries before I hauled them out to their car. Roy and Dorothy instilled in me the need to provide good customer service all of the time.

DANNY DIAMOND SUCCESS TIP:

It is amazing what you can learn and accomplish simply because *someone else* believes you can.

If you are willing to learn, willing to "Expose yourself", there is *always* someone available to teach and pass on their experience.

Roy detailed and demonstrated how to order the product for the store and circulate perishables. He taught me about profit margins and how to build shipping costs into the pricing. I learned that cash flow was king and how improved cash flow can make for a much happier owner. Eventually, I was able to run the store without Roy or Dorothy which, I am happy to say, they took advantage of a few times. I worked for the Dayman's for 7 years. It wasn't work really. It was an education.

All of these people and businesses were part of my early network and gave me lessons that I use personally and in my businesses to this day.

I am betting that most everyone could relate early job experiences that influence aspects of how they operate personally, in their career or in their business today. If your first jobs were babysitting, mowing lawns, shovelling snow off driveways, or cleaning cars in the neighbourhood, then you were self-employed. Think back to your very first job working for a business. Did they ever talk about customer service? Or about waste increasing expenses? Or the importance of being on time? Hopefully they shared profit margins as well so that you knew what made the store the most amount of money. How well did you operate and perform? Did any of the "lessons" carry over to today?

How do you operate now? How well do you mind your business?

The departments in a business model are Accounting, Human Resources, Purchasing, Sales and Marketing, and Operations. All of these exist in one's personal life, one's personal business, as well.

- Accounting: some do it better than others but most everybody keeps records of money coming in and money going out. And most produce a statement of accounts for the Government each year.

- Human Resources: is about recruitment, training, health and safety, and company pay structures. Just like any HR department: We constantly recruit new people into our network. We take courses (training) both personally and at work. We establish health, car, house and life insurance. And we constantly strive for appropriate pay structure.

- Purchasing: most of us do not have a problem making purchases. We typically buy all of the necessities plus a whole lot more.

- Sales and Marketing: we all like to socialize and tell stories, which is marketing to our network. We sell things to people (cars, houses, etc.) and no matter what we do for a living, it is designed to get, keep and satisfy customers for us or for somebody else.

- Operations: In our personal lives, the operations department works 24/7, especially if kids are involved. This department is centered on personal and family schedule and that the highest quality products like home and lifestyle, are produced.

So everyone is running a business whether they think they do or not or treat it as such.

THE DESPERATION FACTOR

Both personally and professionally you are a project initiator who utilizes and manages a network of contacts, associates and mentors for time, money, and expertise. You talk about, plan for and start new projects almost every day. Then spend a lot of time trying to figure out how you can afford the time and money for the projects to become successes.

You are an entrepreneur by default.

Risk:

"We start running risks when we get out of bed in the morning. There is no growth of any kind without risk. Risks are good for us. They bring out the best in us. They brighten the eye and get the mind cooking. They quicken the step and put a shiny new look on our days. Human beings should never be settled. People start to die when they are settled. We need to keep things stirred up."

—**Earl Nightingale, Author of "The Strangest Secret"**

Business people and entrepreneurs, like you are, take risks. Risk creates what I like to call "The Desperation Factor".

I don't mean desperation in its normal definition or context, which revolves around recklessness, loss of hope, unplanned, unorganized, etc. I use **desperation** in the context of desire; of courage born of desperation; of the "juice", the pizzazz, the "umph", the energy that flows because a desperate or high risk state exists. The "doing" because **not doing** would mean a consequence that is much worse than doing the work necessary to make something a success.

As an example, from the last Chapter, Andrew was throwing away the keys to his business. However, Andrew's "Desperation Factor", the negative consequences of walking away – facing his customers and his daughter - became very high compared to the hard work involved in rolling up his sleeves to turn things around. It was only when he *exposed* himself (i.e. asked for help from his network) that he learned he wasn't by himself or had to do it all by himself.

For any project a person walks away from, be it a major purchase with life savings on the line or falling off a diet or workout program, the "Desperation Factor" is not high enough to do what is necessary to make the project successful.

DANNY DIAMOND SUCCESS TIP:

It has always amazed me that many people will invest life savings into a business, yet won't do the things necessary, or utilize the resources available, that experience and history show are the factors that make for a successful business. Simply stated, their "Desperation Factor" is not high enough.

My recommendation before accepting failure, in any area of your life, is to take advantage of one of your most precious resources, your Networking Ooh La La! list, and expose yourself and your plans to people in your network. Help will come, because it always does, and your "Desperation Factor", the desire and pride to turn things around, will increase significantly.

In keeping that everyone is in business and an entrepreneur, the table below shows some of the preferences in personal, career and business opportunity. Although meant to be a generalization, there are points in each of the categories that stand out - money as a priority being one of them.

There is a "rich" myth about business ownership. "If you own a business, you must be rich" (hence the number one answer being *money* when people are asked why they want to get into business). But before the "rich" part happens, there is a lot of hard work involved. The deterrent to "rich" is explained in another point that stands out in all of the categories; that being, taking the necessary action.

Business Opportunities	Job/Career Opportunities	Personal Opportunities
Prefer existing systems (don't have to reinvent the wheel).	gravitate to or prefer existing business systems	Tend to gravitate to existing consumer systems and brands for our needs and desires.
Want good operating hours, marketing, strong brand, good validation from existing franchisees.	Looking for good hours, a strong brand & validation from existing employees.	We market (socialize, what we're doing); have a brand (reputation); get validation from others (our integrity).
Money is always the #1 answer as to why people get into business, then lifestyle. Must have the time, money and desire, to take the business system and the opportunity to the marketplace.	Money is one of the biggest factors, while the employer's priority is someone who has the time and desire to compliment and assist with the offering to the marketplace.	Money is one of the biggest factors. As consumers, we aren't taking opportunities to the marketplace. Instead, we desire and strive *for* the time and money to take advantage of the opportunities in the marketplace.
Challenges to business success: 1) looking to buy a job instead of running a business; 2) want to make money & lots of it, right away; and, 3) not willing to do the marketing & other proven procedures necessary to tell enough people about their great offering.	Challenges to job/career success: 1) focussed on "what's in it for me"; 2) want to make money and more money; 3) not willing to do the procedures/actions necessary to assist the company to get, keep and satisfy more customers.	Challenges to personal success: 1) focussed more on spending than saving; 2) they want more money, and lots of it, right away (to buy more things); 3) an unwillingness to take risks and the action necessary to attain their goals and desires.

We are all customers

From a Business Opportunity perspective:

What kind of experience do we want the customer to have? What influences our customers to come back? What does the customer expect when the telephone is answered? What does the customer expect when they walk into a busy store? What does the customer say about a business that provides a solution for them?

If the focus, the "Desperation Factor" if you will, about and for the customer is high enough, everything else in the business – accounting, human resources, marketing, sales, purchasing, operations – all take on an *about and for the customer* purpose automatically. Sound pretty simple?

 DANNY DIAMOND SUCCESS TIP:

If the business is solely focussed on money, it makes success a bigger struggle. Why? Because it is the *customer* who has the money for what the business offers and the solutions the business provides.

Focus on the customer and the money will come automatically.

We are all customers.

From a Career/Job Opportunity perspective:

If you were a customer of the company you work for, ask yourself: What kind of experience would you want to have? What would influence you to come back? What would you expect when the telephone is answered when you call? What would you expect when you walk in on a busy day? What would you say about the business if it provided the solution you were looking for?

For more career and job success, try thinking like the customer.

Because of the constant quest for money, people stay in jobs they don't like, or continuously move from job to job. The general feeling of most employees is that the company owes them. Instead they were hired to make the company money - by providing the accounting, human resources, sales and marketing, purchasing, or operations necessary, to get, keep and satisfy customers. For this the company is prepared and obligated to share the customer's money with the employees.

If you choose to focus your daily work, *for and about the customer*, everything else about your position – recognition, raises, promotions, etc. – will come naturally.

 DANNY DIAMOND SUCCESS TIP:

Similar to a business focussing only on the money and making success a bigger struggle than it needs to be, the same is true with a career or job.

Focus on money instead of the customer makes everything a bigger struggle..

Why?

Because, whether it is your business or someone else's, it is the *customer* who has the money for what the company offers and the solutions the company provides. Do everything with a *focus on the customer* and the money, your share of the customer's money, will come automatically and in bigger quantities.

YOUR PERSONAL BUSINESS MINDSET:

The only real reason to have a business, career or job is for the betterment of your personal lifestyle, personal opportunity and what I like to call, **Your Personal Business**.

Your Personal Business, gets, keeps and satisfies customers just like a regular business does. Only your "customers" are disguised as family, friends, associates, colleagues, mentor... everyone on your Networking Ooh La La! list.

Keep your focus on getting, keeping and satisfying everyone possible in your network - *exposing yourself for success* - and everything you want, need and desire will take care of itself.

Repeating the line, "gets, keeps and satisfies", then replace *customers* with family, then friends, then mentors, etc.

The main purpose of my personal business is to get, keep and satisfy_____.

Every business requires full commitment for success. That means how you operate day to day in your personal life has the same requirement, as you are indeed in business for yourself even if you don't "officially" own a business.

For clarification, as with any business, Your Personal Business:

1. Must be viable with some money left over at the end of the month once all expenses are paid.

2. Must have goods and services, consumer items that are bought and sold (mostly bought) monthly.

3. Must have good staff management in your personal affairs. You empower and manage staff, whether you realize it or not. It could be official staff, as in a housekeeper or gardener, but everyone that helps you get through your day by providing goods and services are really your staff members as well. The grocery store clerk, your dentist, a repairman, your lawyer, your kid's teachers, etc. You pay them and pay them well, and all need to be managed.

4. Is to be of service every day. Your products - you, your family, your household - have incredible value that needs to be nurtured and exposed to your network so that they can be of service to you, as you are of service to them.

5. Is a selling machine. We are all in sales and have been since we were born. As kids, we were the perfect sales people, relentless in asking for everything. As adults, many feel that sales people

are typically aggressive, direct, not believable and insincere. But it is important for you to be good at sales. We sell to the bank when we negotiate a mortgage. We sell to an employer when we apply for a job. We sell to anyone providing services to our household, always looking for the best deal. It may seem like we are the ones being sold to but, as consumers, we are in control. If it wasn't true, companies and industries wouldn't struggle or shut down when consumer buying habits change. You are a sales person. Be the best one you can be, with integrity, honesty, sincerity and, of course, be proud of it. "Ask for the order", so they say. You are not inconveniencing anyone.

6. Has its own full-blown marketing department. Where you are during the day, where you live, what you do daily, who you know, who you promote, who you refer people to, who you get referred to, etc. - it's all marketing. Stories of family, of vacations, of your health, of work, of your business – it's all marketing. At any stage in our lives, the greatest opportunity for both personal and business growth, the real gold, is in marketing.

7. Has systems like any business, developed and designed by you to simplify life as much as possible. Systems create consistency and reliability which creates confidence and kills feelings of "overwhelm" and stress. Systems are influenced by our habits - good or bad. Old, unsupportive habits can be exchanged for new, supportive habits and this is one of the reasons personal business systems are always being tweaked, enhanced, and revised.

8. Is an investment like any business. It is not about consumption or just making ends meet. As with a storefront type business, your personal business has assets, goodwill and inventory. You may have used some leverage and taken on some risk (mortgage, car loan or lease, line of credit) and the affordability of all consumption and purchases should be scrutinized with the intent of maximum return on your personal business investment. Your return on investment is indicated by your

savings, your investments, as well as who you help along the way, who you *can* help if needed, who you mentor. Your return on investment is also retirement, how you have structured it for you and your family and the legacy you leave behind.

EXERCISE 13:

With all of the above in mind, where does your business mindset stand? Do you **Mind Your Business**?

Please answer the questions below to find out. As always, this is you talking to you.

1. Do you have any business experience? _____ Yes _____ No
(After all that you have read in this chapter, the answer better be "Yes")

2. Are you a business owner now? _____ Yes _____ No
If "No", have you ever wanted to own your own business?
_____ Yes _____ No

4. Do you have the financial backing to start a business?
_____ Yes _____ No

5. Do you work well with a team of others? _____ Yes _____ No

6. Are you good with money and finance? _____ Yes _____ No

7. Do you feel you have creative skills? _____ Yes _____ No

8. Are you hard working? _____ Yes _____ No

9. Would you be willing to work harder for potentially less money (at start-up)?

_____ Yes   _____ No

10. Are you prepared to adapt to the needs of your business?

_____ Yes   _____ No

11. Are you motivated?   _____ Yes   _____ No

12. Are you *motivating*?   _____ Yes   _____ No

13. Do you create balance between your personal life and work?

_____ Yes   _____ No

14. Would you be able to adjust to a possible fluctuating income, rather than a set salary and standard pay cheque?   _____ Yes   _____ No

15. Do you have management skills?   _____ Yes   _____ No

16. Do you have the ability to train others?   _____ Yes   _____ No

17. Do you have support from family and friends – **your network**?

_____ Yes   _____ No

18. Do you have a mentor, someone you can take advice and learn from or model?

_____ Yes   _____ No

19. Do you adapt to new technology well? _____ Yes _____ No

20. Are you open to new ideas? _____ Yes _____ No

21. Do you believe in yourself? _____ Yes _____ No

22. Have you created a big enough "Desperation Factor" in your life to propel your success? _____ Yes _____ No

If "No", do you recognize the importance of a "Desperation Factor" which creates the unwillingness to accept failure (as in the example of Andrew and his business)? _____ Yes _____ No

24. Are you a sales person? _____ Yes _____ No

25. Are you comfortable promoting yourself everyday in every way?
_____ Yes _____ No

Count up your "**Yes's**". If you answered "**Yes**" to:

21-25 questions, your Business Mindset is on track for maximum success;

11-20 questions, the potential is there, expose yourself more to your network. They are waiting to help you;

1-10 questions, you may be standing in your own way. Action trumps everything. Take more action. Help is only an "ask" away.

EXERCISE #14:

"How Money Leaves The Building"

DANNY DIAMOND SUCCESS TIP (REPRISE):

This "how money leaves the building" analysis works just as well for personal finances as it does for business finances.

If you ever feel you are struggling with cash flow personally, do a financial analysis to discover exactly "how money leaves the building". Then, do what Andrew did - use your network to work on solutions for making the 180 degree turn.

This is the Profit & Loss, the Income, the Viability part of Your Personal Business life. It sets the tone for and enhances your business mindset, even if you are not a fan of numbers and number crunching. It is something one should do quarterly at the very minimum.

For many, this may be an "exposure". A realization, a learning, a "wake-up call", as it was for Andrew. For others, it will be a review and a great time to update your latest numbers. At the very least, it will be a good exercise in relocating and organizing necessary information and files.

Get help if you need it. If you are the one that usually does the financial end of things, then let someone else in the family do it, while you assist. If the one in your family who keeps track of the finances normally doesn't share, this is the time to call a family meeting and share. Once you complete the exercise, you will have a very valuable tool and resource to share with family and those you most trust in your network.

Over the years, through my business, seminars and workshops, I have witnessed and worked with hundreds of people, even seasoned business owners, who either do not understand their personal and/or business finances or, simply are not comfortable crunching the numbers. Even those individuals that have hired a bookkeeper or outsourced this responsibility fall into this category, and this amazes me.

It is so important. If you track it, you will attract it.

And if this exercise makes you feel uncomfortable, perfect. It is the right exercise for you.

> *"Behold the turtle. He makes progress*
> *only when he sticks his neck out."*

—Unknown

PERSONAL INCOME AND EXPENSE SHEET

Fill in all the income sources that apply to you. Then enter all expenses that apply to you. Your Personal Profit = Total Income – Total Expenses

Name:_____   Date: _____

	Monthly Budget
Income:	
Primary Income	
Spouse's Income	
Child Support or Alimony	
Unemployment Income	
Disability Income	
Pension Income	
Investment Income (after expenses)	
Real Estate Investment Income (after expenses)	
Business Income (after expenses)	
Other Income	
Total Income	
Expenses:	
Rent or Mortgage	
Home Equity Loan	
Property Taxes	
Utilities	
Water	
Garbage	
Gas Company	
Electric	
Total Utilities	

Automobile
    Insurance
    Registration
    Repair & Maintenance
    Loans & Leases
    Fuel
        Total Automobile
Food & Groceries
Clothing
Clothing Children
Telephone
    Home
    Cellular/Mobile
        Total Telephone
Insurance
    Home/Renters
    Medical/Healthcare
    Dental
    Life
        Total Insurance
Entertainment
    Cable/Satellite TV
    Dining Out
    Vacation & Travel
    Movies
    Movie Rentals
    Other
        Total Entertainment
Household
    Home Repair/Maintenance.
    Home supplies
    Home Improvement
    Security
    Garden Supplies
    Computer Expenses
    Internet Service
        Total Household
Investment
    Retirement Accounts
    Stocks
    Mutual Funds
    Other
        Total Investment
Childcare (daycare & babysitters)
Student Loans
Pet Costs
Other Expenses

        Total Expenses

        Personal Profit (Loss)

NET WORTH STATEMENT (PAGE 1 OF 2)

If you sold everything you owned today, at today's price (not what you paid for it); then paid off everything you owed; the amount of money left over is your net worth.

Assets	Amount in Dollars
Cash - checking accounts	$ _____
Cash - savings accounts	_____
Certificates of deposit	_____
Loans/contracts receivable (from Page 2)	_____
Securities - stocks / bonds / mutual funds (from Page 2)	_____
Life insurance (cash surrender value)	_____
Personal property (autos, jewellery, etc.)	_____
Retirement Funds (e.g. RRSP, IRAs, 401k) from Page 2	_____
Real estate (market value) from Page 2	_____
Other assets (specify)	_____
Other assets (specify)	_____
Total Assets	$ _____

Liabilities	Amount in Dollars
Current Debt (Credit cards, Accounts) from Page 2	$ ____ - ____
Loans/Lines of Credit payable (from Page 2)	____ - ____
Taxes payable	____ - ____
Real estate mortgages (from Page 2)	____ - ____
Other liabilities (specify)	____ - ____
Other liabilities (specify)	____ - ____
Total Liabilities	$ ____ - ____
Net Worth	$ ____ - ____

Net Worth Statement (Page 2 of 2)

1. ASSET DETAILS

Loans/Contracts Receivables

Name	Balance Owing	Original Amount	Start Date	Monthly Pay-ment
	$	$		$

Retirement Accounts/Holdings

Name/Type	No. of Shares	Cost	Market Value	Date Acquired
		$	$	

Securities: stocks / bonds / mutual funds

Name of Security	No. of Shares	Cost	Market Value	Date Acquired
		$	$	

Real Estate

Description / Location	Market Value	Amount Owing	Original Cost	Purchase Date
	$	$	$	

2. LIABILITIES DETAILS

Credit Card Debt

Name of Card / Creditor	Amount Due
	$

Loans, Line of Credit

Name of Creditor	Amount Owing	Original Amount	Monthly Pay-ment	Interest Rate
	$	$	$	

Mortgage / Real Estate Loans Payable

Name of Creditor	Amount Owing	Original Amount	Monthly Pay-ment	Interest Rate
	$	$	$	

The Personal Financial Statement and Personal Income & Expense Sheet templates are available at www.thecolourofmyunderwearisblue.com

Congratulations for completing this exercise.

How did it go? Was your net worth as high as you thought it was? Was your Personal Profit monthly as much as you thought it would be, or hoped for? Is there money left at the end of the month?

Did you discover how money leaves the building? Are there any areas you have discovered that adjustments need to be made?

What expenses could you do away with to improve the bottom line? Could you eat out less? Buy fewer clothes? Are your automobile costs too high? Are you directing enough to investments?

What could be done to increase the income portion of the profit and loss statement?

Is there anything you are willing to give up if it meant you could realize your goals and desires much faster?

The truth of the matter is, you will have to sacrifice some things that are not in direct alignment with your goals and desires.

Think of it as opening space, clearing the way, and making room in order to provide the opportunity to stretch and grow towards your life dreams.

By completing this exercise you have two very valuable documents that can be used to accelerate your success. Do what Andrew did. Take the results as a call to action and ask for help. Use it to "Expose Yourself for Success".

Congratulations for being a business person, and entrepreneur. Congratulations on Minding Your Business.

CHAPTER 8:

– Forget Your Way To Success – From
Incremental to Exponential –

"There is a difference between interest and commitment. When you are interested in doing something, you do it only when it is convenient. When you are committed to something, you accept no excuses, only results."

—Kenneth Blanchard, Ph.D.

"Give me a lever long enough and I could move the world."

—Archimedes.

LYON ON LEVERAGE:

One afternoon at Barons Consolidated High School, my sister's and older brother's grades 5 and 6 classes (which was Miss Sonmor's class if you may remember from Chapter 1) laid out a snare for a gopher at the school. Not at recess but during classroom time. They tied all of their shoelaces together to make the snare and then ran it out the first floor window, down to the ground and across the lawn to the gopher hole in the front school yard, by the flagpole. Remember, this was during class. What teamwork they possessed!

They got caught because a teacher on the second floor, while looking out the window during a lecture, spotted something mysterious on the front lawn. I believe both grades, all of them, got the strap. Hopefully both teachers and students did not miss the teamwork that was involved on the project and the massive use of leverage – time, people, secrecy, common purpose, shared risk, procedures, promotion and, of course, borrowed shoe laces.

Discussions around leverage are most times financial discussions. Financial leverage is utilized any time money is borrowed for the purchase of anything – a car, a house, home renovation loan, vacation loan, line of credit, an investment property, investment portfolio, a business, etc. The main purpose of financial leverage is to improve the possible rate of return on an investment, and there is higher risk as well.

But in today's world, we as consumers like to use financial leverage for personal purchases as opposed to just investment purchases. Cars, trips and personal purchases through credit cards and lines of credit don't improve the rate of return on *any* investment. You can't sell the trip you just enjoyed. The return on investment of personal purchases is really zero, yet we leverage ourselves to buy them.

Leverage does not have to be financial.

Although financial leverage is important and important to understand, my preference is to focus on a much more powerful form of leverage…**people leverage**. In fact, I dare say that anyone in a less than desired financial situation can get more support and in a better position much quicker by utilizing people leverage – their network.

It is what you have been working on throughout this book. There are people in your network or people who want to come into your network that can assist you with any financial issue, or know of someone that can, and get you pointed in the right direction. It is ***exposing yourself for success*** and letting the power of your network support you.

DANNY DIAMOND SUCCESS TIP:

For any specific problem, task or goal at hand – be it financial or otherwise - until a person is willing to stretch their current comfort zone around exposing themselves and exposing the issue to their network, they don't fully know:

- Who is already in their network that can help?

- Who has been hovering just inside the borders of their comfort zone waiting to be asked to help?

- Who hasn't even been thought of yet because they weren't visible on the other side of the comfort zone boundary?

A few of the things that can be leveraged and already exist in your network are:

Money	Time	Information
Knowledge	Expertise	Contacts
Relationships	Credibility	Reputation
Products	Services	Procedures
Location	Facilities	Assets
Delegation	Duplication	Systems
Partnerships	Joint Ventures	Strategic Alliances
Effective marketing	Other people's money	Licensing
Technology	Database	Database Management
Customers	Inventory	Goodwill

The above list is a personal asset of yours, available at your beck and call if you choose to capitalize on them. All of us, no matter how much we feel we are team players and currently utilize our network, are sitting on a great resource – our ever changing, ever expanding Networking Ooh

La La! list - that can explode any of us from incremental to exponential success. We just have to get out of our own way.

Your network has the power to lessen the learning curve for anything and remove barriers, both real and perceived. This network of yours is loaded with experience and expertise and is willing to share it. They just need to know you, know you better and, most importantly, they need to know you're what you want.

Just how powerful and influential can your network be?

It is your **ultimate resource.**

EXERCISE 15:

Without thinking too hard, list 5 events on your journey through life so far that were perhaps life changing, because someone in your network got to know you better or you shared your plans with them. There are many events, as there are for everyone. The first 5 that came to me when thinking about this were:

1. **Grandfather** - Upon several discussions and encouragement from my grandfather, I finally accepted the risk of rejection and drove into Lethbridge to try out for a "city" baseball team. Result: I went to my first national championship that year and went to nationals 3 times over the years.

2. **Colleagues** - After talking to several colleagues who had worked on telecom projects outside of Canada, I submitted my name into the resource pool. I was 28 years old, had only been out of the Province of Alberta a few times and on an airplane twice in my life. Result: Six years of working throughout the U.S. plus projects in Guam, Puerto Rico and Brazil. This was followed by four years in Thailand.

3. **Friend** - Discussing with a friend about Connie Campbell being a member of our mixed curling team. He knew her well, I didn't. Result: It took a lot of work to get her to say "yes" but The Beautiful and Vivacious Mrs. Connie Lyon and I have been happily married for over 20 years and have Tommy, Davey and Maggie.

4. **Business people** (new to my network) - Sending questionnaires to 12 Franchisees across Canada, their validation helped complete our due diligence on the Mail Boxes Etc. franchise. Result: We successfully owned our store for 10 years and we have been in the business for more than 14 years now .

5. **Presenter** (new to my network) - After seeing bestselling author Cynthia Kersey present on the Bob Proctor Cruise, I "borrowed" her birthday model for fundraising. Result: We raised enough money to build a school in Kenya and travelled there with my son, Davey, to help build the classrooms and spend time in the villages learning about the great people of the Maasai Mara.

Grab a piece of paper.

Take a minute and think of some of the directions you took in your life, some of the things you accomplished, as a result of taking the initiative to share or talk to someone in your network.

Don't think too much.

Just relax and let them come to you.

Now write them down.

Person	Event, Opportunity Discussed	What did you do to act on what you learned?	Result
1)			
2)			

3)			
4)			
5)			

EXERCISE 16:

From your Networking Ooh La La! list, pick five people in your network today that **you know** you should be talking to but haven't made contact with yet. People **you know** can help you with some of your wants, needs, goals and desires.

If it makes you uncomfortable to do this, perfect. It is the right exercise for you.

Take the chance, walk to the edge of the cliff (pick up the phone, make the call and set up a meeting), and let them know who you are and what you want.

The chart below may be of assistance to get you started.

Take action and your results will move from incremental to exponential.

"If you aren't living on the edge,
then you are taking up too much room."

—**Bob Proctor**

* Note: a template of this form is available at
www.thecolourofmyunderwearisblue.com

Name of the Person You Know You Should Talk To	What is the subject you want to discuss? What do you want their help with? (your want, need, goal or desire)	What is the date you are committed to calling or contacting them by? (the shorter the time frame the better)	Write in the date of the scheduled call or meeting with this person.
Example: Frank Wallace	I want to lose 30lbs by summer. What lifestyle changes do you suggest?	January 15th	January 20th
1)			
2)			
3)			
4)			
5)			

* * * * * * * * * * * * *

WARNING!!!

In dealing with your network, you are going to get good at:

- **taking action** on connecting regularly
- masterminding with them
- expanding your network
- consistently exposing yourself and your plans
- being open to the advice and mentoring provided
- **taking action** on the ideas and opportunities provided

Be prepared to take off on an exhilarating, fast-paced journey that leaves many people behind - even those close to you.

* * * * * * * * * * * * *

My network dynamic has changed many times over the years. Everyone's does. One of the most significant periods of network change and expansion was the years I travelled outside of the country with telecommunications. The pace, what I saw and experienced, the people I met, the increased awareness of what was out there and the opportunities that existed; were sometimes difficult to share back home. Security bars on my 9th story hotel windows in Puerto Rico, a drug related shooting of a security guard at one of the tiny telecom sites I was working at in Brazil, 100+ protesting students being shot by the army in Bangkok just a couple of miles from where we were sitting, seeing the Cubs play the Dodgers at Wrigley Field in the afternoon, then driving to south Chicago to see the White Sox play the Yankees in the evening game. Things that don't happen in Lethbridge and that had to compete with issues like *the* pothole on 3rd Ave.

The disconnect was me. I was away so much that the pot hole, probably the same one that used to drive me nuts too, couldn't be related to anymore. Not surprisingly, I naturally gravitated to people, many of them new to my network who supported my travels and I naturally moved away from those that wanted me to stop the travelling (and probably get refocused on the pothole).

Happily, I still live in Lethbridge, Alberta, Canada and do so because a pothole can make front page news. I have learned that my focus and vision can remain beyond a pothole and that my network is ever expanding and supportive.

The same disconnect can happen to you on your road to success.

"A rising tide lifts all boats."

—**Proverb**

Some in your network may wonder where you have gone as you ascend your stairway to success but you didn't really go anywhere. You are on your new path and they are still on their old path. You just leveraged your network to take you to a different level of experience, and new awareness of possibilities. You may even be helping others enjoy their own journey from incremental to exponential success.

It becomes the choice of those who feel they are left behind to accept or reject the new you. Many will try to haul you back down to earth, to put concrete shoes on your feet, back to where you fit into *their* comfort zone. Stay the course. Focus. Don't let them bring you back. Ensure your "Desperation Factor" is high enough that your results and potential for more successes far outweigh dropping back into your old comfort zone. Way more people want to be around for the ride with the new rising tide, **you.**

DANNY DIAMOND SUCCESS TIP:

To maximize people leverage through your network – really, to maximize *anything* on your road to success – you have to grab a bat and come to the plate swinging.

It is hard to get a hit if you never leave the dugout.

And if you do come to the plate, it is hard to get a hit if you *never take the bat off your shoulder.* Swing, batta, batta, swing!

You don't need to hit a home run. Those that think you do and those that swing for the fence strike out a lot. Many have never seen first base.

You just need to swing. Swing without being embarrassed or worrying about striking out.

The hits will come. Your coaches, your network, will help you hit better and better each time up.

But they can't make you step up to the plate. You have to do that.

FORGET IT!

In almost everything I have tried, I always wanted to know as much as possible and tried to be the expert "doer". I will be the first to admit that I am not even close to being the expert on anything – especially marriage and kids (but I am still studying profusely).

I worked hard in learning and *doing* - as a student, as an athlete and as a telecom technician.

I have always bragged that I am very coachable and I have always felt I was a "doer" type on any team or project.

When Connie and I made the decision to move forward with a Mail Boxes Etc. Franchise in October, 1995 and open a store in Lethbridge, we had a master plan. We were going to go on one more out of country telecom project. The kids were small and my sister Penny was available to manage and run the store. After the completion of the project, we were going to settle back in Lethbridge and become shop-keeps of our Mail Boxes Etc. I even had a shower built into the bathroom of the store. The intent was to run to the store in the mornings, shower, work the business, and run back home at the end of the day.

The master plan changed when we decided to stay in Canada.

I switched and did the same as I had done with everything else – learn the procedures, follow the rules and capitalize on other's shared experience to do the best job possible; to be the "doer". I took all of the Franchisee training with Penny. I worked in the store daily for a few months. I did the bookkeeping and did the marketing with Connie. If by some stretch of the imagination everyone left us, I would have been able to take over all operations in a heartbeat.

That is how my business life started. It soon turned into an education on what I call "**Forget Your Way to Success**".

Something very interesting happened. Several months later, I was no longer an Owner/Operator. For the first time, my "doer" tendencies as a technician were not needed and, quite frankly, they had eroded quickly. I was now an Owner only and to ever work on the service counter again I would need to be retrained. The events leading to this were:

- A manager (Penny) and sales associates (my nieces Lisa and Jaclyn) were in place before we ever opened. I never really was needed on the service counter, right from the get-go. We were fortunate to have great sales associates throughout the whole time we owned the store.

- My focus was on marketing. With life savings on the line, the "Desperation Factor" was created for us just as it would be for most people. In our minds, and we assumed it was the same for anyone starting a new business, telling the world about our offering and building a large customer base seemed too logical. Getting, keeping and satisfying customers, was what our "Desperation Factor" drove us towards.

- We made a couple of unsuccessful attempts to expand to more stores.

- Because I wasn't needed at the store day to day, I accepted the occasional short term telecom project. First in Southern Alberta, then in the U.S.

- The final event was when we accepted the opportunity to purchase the Area Franchise rights for the Provinces of Alberta and Saskatchewan from the existing owner. My sister-in-law Kathy made the decision to partner with us.

Conversion from Shop-keep to Owner created a new "Desperation Factor".

What if everyone working at the store left? I was going to be away a lot more and who would run the store if they all walked out?

Attention switched to systems, operations, training and, most importantly, staff empowerment and responsibility. Connie and Lisa led the way in planning and implementation. They empowered the staff with responsibility and the result was a very slow turnover rate and remarkable loyalty.

It took 4 offers over 10 months and at the end of September, 1998, we took over the Area as well as the previous Area Franchisee's store in Calgary. My days were now filled with a myriad of new duties. I was now doing the books for two stores, helping Kathy oversee operations at the store in Calgary, meet new candidates looking at the Franchise, all the while learning the responsibilities of Area Franchisee-ism. The "Forget It" process concerning my knowledge of working on the counter was now at full throttle.

An example of this is a story that Kathy likes to tell to everyone in the system. There was a line-up at the store in Calgary, despite 3 good people working the counter, including Kathy. I was in the back doing the books when Kathy asked me to come out and help. I greeted the first couple and asked all of the right questions concerning their shipment. (Could it be I still had "it"?) They wanted to ship their package by FedEx. I tried my best to find the FedEx waybills in the slots under the counter but couldn't. Not wanting to disturb Kathy or the others too much, with my hands on my hips and slightly bent over still looking, I casually said (a little too loud), "If I were a FedEx waybill, where would I be?" Kathy promptly sent me to the back of the store announcing that I was hindering not helping. It was December 1998 and that was my last "on the counter" work in a store.

Many months later, at one of the networking meetings we host quarterly, a Franchisee interrupted my presentation with the challenge that, 'you are the one presenting but you don't even know the proper forms for certain (courier) shipments to the states. How can you be helping us?' Wow, an honest and very valid question. Even though shipping forms were not related to what I was presenting at the time, my answer was, "How many would like to forget about shipping forms and have a successful business without working the front counter anymore?" Everyone raised their hand.

And that is what I could help with.

Sales in our store in Lethbridge did not peak until 2002, 4 years after I stopped working the counter. Yes it was because of great managers and great sales associates. The store ran better without my day to day involvement in operations. These are good things. The new "Desperation Factor" helped create:

- monthly staff meetings where the staff members set the agenda, not us;

- creation of departments –different staff members were now in charge of mailboxes, the main database, the email database, supply orders, receivable posting, even though we were only an 1100 square foot store; and

- training procedures and systems for new staff.

I have always felt that The "Desperation Factor" kept the focus on business planning, business development and the most important aspect of any business, marketing. Tell 'em all, tell 'em often and they will come.

I realized I had made a mistake. My loss of technical skills in the store hadn't created an Owner only. The loss of those skills created a businessman. I had forgotten my way to success and didn't even know it.

Around summer 2000 I got reacquainted with Michael Gerber's book, The E-Myth Revisited. Since I was no longer the technician in my store in Lethbridge, The E-Myth Revisited really hit home this time, more so than the previous time I had read it. Promoting to new and existing business owners that they run their business like a business, and helping them with that, became my *thing* - because I had experienced it. Also around that same summer, I became very interested in personal development and went through all of the programs offered by T. Harv Eker and Peak Potentials. Along the journey in Harv's programs, I met an extraordinary gentleman by the name of Andrew Barber-Starkey. I have been a part of Andrew's business and personal coaching program since then, including the last 4 years in his Inner Circle mastermind group. These influences have all helped me maintain and believe in the promotion of running a business like a business.

As in business, a lot of time can be consumed being "everything" everyday as opposed to keeping the main thing the main thing – focus on your dreams and desires. Some may argue that by saving dollars on doing projects themselves helped them stay headed towards their goals. A valid point perhaps. Maybe doing all of your own oil changes helped save enough money for the boat or cottage that might be on your dreams list. But I wonder how much closer we might get to our goals if we cut down on the number of projects we take on? What if we handed some projects over to professionals to complete for us? I think it is good to be budget conscious. However, if the freed up time and stress of being the "doer" creates more opportunities to grow and succeed, can budget consciousness limit what we say we want to accomplish? I think so. Use of *people leverage* to get at least some of these things done provides us with the freedom to grow (as long as one keeps the main thing moving forward and doesn't just flop on the couch).

We still need to be action takers. However, our actions need to be geared towards fulfillment of our life dreams and not just working on personal projects that save money but cost dearly in time.

EXERCISE 17: *Unfinished Projects*

* Note: a template of this form is available at www.thecolourofmyunderwearisblue.com

In the table below list 5-10 projects that are at various stages in your personal life and are stagnant because you don't have the resources – time, money, desire, etc. – to complete.

Then, indicate if they would be better off in someone else's hands.

When doing this exercise, don't worry if there is enough money around to pay for another person to complete the project. Just be objective on whether you feel it would be better off in someone else's hands.

If money IS the hold up, is there anything that could be done differently (expenses saved, sell something, change investments, etc.) that could provide some extra revenue such that sufficient funding for the project is attained? Please note, if part of the solution is to use someone else's knowledge, please write their name in this section. Then contact them.

Unfinished Project/Task	Would this be better off in someone else's hands?	Is money the hold back to hiring someone? If so, what could I do to lessen expenses or improve cash flow such that I can hire someone? What is the name of someone I could be talking to?
Example: paint the living room	Yes, definitely	Yes. Cancel magazine subscriptions; cut out some entertainment expenses; look at new cell phone package. Set up a family meeting to discuss priorities. Contact Joel to look at increased returns on our investments.

1)		
2)		
3)		
4)		
5)		
6)		
7)		
8)		
9)		
10)		

Leverage is power!

Utilizing people leverage is powerful. For exponential success, maximizing the great network you have at your disposal is essential. They are already there. By now, you know your network can help you *get on the right path*. They can also help you get things done without you having to do them yourself - so that you can *stay on the right path*.

Don't worry about what you don't know or what you forget along the way. Your network knows all.

Congratulations on completing the exercises in Chapter 8!

Congratulations to you on your great network and for letting them support you at every turn!

CHAPTER 9:

– Motivate the Motivator –

There's a great joy in my giving. It's thrilling. It's exhilarating.
It's important to be a part of sharing. It is my love. It is my joy.

—W. Clement Stone

Givers Gain. I have heard it countless times.

Givers Gain because they expand, utilize and help their network when they give.

We make a living by what we get,
but we make a life by what we give.

—Sir Winston Churchill

If you want to motivate someone, show them how much you give and involve them in the process.

If you want to motivate yourself, review how much you give and are involved with the giving process. A great place to start is back in Chapter 1 with who is in your network, who you have inspired, who has inspired you, and who you are utilizing on your way to success. Also, re-do the exercises in Chapter 2 with the focus on your "giving" successes. There will be a lot of them.

I believe we are all givers and that our whole existence is about helping others.

Sometimes we get trapped into the rut of only focussing on ourselves and our problems. The fastest way out of any "rut" is to give. In my experience, there is nothing as "feel good" as helping someone else.

 DANNY DIAMOND SUCCESS TIP:

If you want more motivation for yourself, then give.

If you want to be more prosperous, more successful – both monetarily and in your soul – then give.

If you want to leapfrog to exponential success, just give.

Give your time, give your money, give your expertise, give your experience.

Coach a team. Volunteer – at the food shelter, on a non-profit board of directors, at your kid's school. Write a cheque for something if you can.

The more you give the more motivated you will be. The better the energy will be. The better *your* energy will be.

As W. Clement Stone said, "It's thrilling. It's exhilarating."

EMOTIONAL INFLUENCE AND PROVIDING A FOUNDATION OF POTENTIAL.

For my 50th birthday, The Beautiful and Vivacious Mrs. Connie Lyon provided a $100 bill to each of 10 close friends and relatives, with the instructions to donate to a worthy cause in my name, in honour of my birthday. I didn't know that she had done this. The only thing I knew was that I didn't get any presents to open on the day of my 50th birthday. I was soon to learn that she had given me the best present ever.

Connie had provided only one guideline for these 10 people (who we affectionately refer to as the "Pay It Forward 10"). After they made the donation they had to visit us at our house, set up a meeting with me, or contact me directly by phone to detail for me what they had done.

The first phone call received was a month after my birthday, from a great friend and mentor to me, Don (Kat) Keturakis. Talk about a "giver". There aren't too many minutes of any day that goes by where Kat is not helping someone. His "you-can-do-it" attitude is very infectious and inspiring. My kids call him Uncle Kat. That is how special he is to our family. Kat was still travelling around the globe testing fibre optic telecom systems as we had done together for many years. As we caught up on things in his telecom world and our franchising world, Kat mentioned that he had donated some money to his favourite charity, 'The Mustard Seed' in Calgary, Alberta (www.theseed.ca). During all of the catching up, I missed the boat completely that the donation he made was with the $100 Connie provided, which he matched with his own money, and was made in my honour for my 50th. We said good-bye and I carried on in oblivion (which I have been accused of many times by my teenage kids).

The second call came from Billy Batdorf. Billy has one of the most infectious laughs on the planet, which accompanies a great sense of humour and a huge giving heart. We also had worked together for years throughout the U.S. and in Thailand on fibre optic systems. When Billy called, we were both pretty excited to catch up on work, family, business, etc. In the midst of all of this excitement and quick conversation, he shared a story about some lady in Costa Rica who he had loaned money to. My first thoughts were why he would be mixed up with a woman he hardly knew from Costa Rica. Before I could get further clarification, poor cellular phone coverage forced a good-bye with a promise to stay in touch more frequently.

A week later, just as I was opening an envelope from The Mustard Seed, Connie asked me if I had heard from anyone special lately. I said, "What a coincidence. I just talked to Kat a week ago and he mentioned that his favourite charity is The Mustard Seed." Then I read the thank-you card below from the Executive Director of The Mustard Seed:

"The Mustard Seed Street Ministry
Gratefully acknowledges a Donation from
Don Ketruakis
Made in honour of your 50th birthday
to provide meals, shelter and other essential services
to Calgary's less fortunate."

Although I questioned Connie for an explanation, she insisted I call Kat for clarification. At this same time, I mentioned to Connie that I had also heard from Billy Batdorf about a mysterious lady Billy had loaned money to in Costa Rica.

The next week I was travelling and took some time to read through all of the information that had come from The Mustard Seed. What an amazing program they have. I was trying to track down Kat for an explanation on why he would donate to The Mustard Seed in my name when I received a call from the very amazing Master Certified Coach, Andrew Barber-Starkey. Andrew has been my business coach, mentor and friend since 2000. Andrew is the creator and facilitator of our Inner Circle mastermind group and his whole life is pretty much dedicated to giving and helping others become successful.

Andrew said, "The money that Connie gave me is posing a challenge to us on where to donate it and we thought it should go back to you. Because you love sports, we thought there might be an athlete in the Lethbridge Area that could benefit from it."

What Money?

Andrew became the first to explain to me that Connie had provided him with $100 to donate to a worthy cause in my name for my 50th. WOW! I was blown away that she had done that for me. Andrew went on to say that he didn't feel $100 was going to have much impact so he matched it with $100 of his own, plus $100 from his company, ProCoach International Ltd. He then invited the other 7 members of our Inner Circle mastermind group to contribute $100 each. And they did, bringing the total to $1,000. Andrew said he would mail a cheque and that I should start looking for a local athlete to help out.

My cluelessness was starting to disappear. I now understood what Kat had been trying to explain to me. Kat and I connected that afternoon and he introduced a great letter from The Mustard Seed Executive Director.

"Thank-you for your gift made in honour of Dan Lyon's 50th birthday. We truly appreciate caring and thoughtful friends like you. This gift will help The SEED continue to provide hot meals, safe shelter, education and work programs to Calgary's less fortunate people, as well as other vital services.

Your support will make a profound difference for our community's neediest men and women. You see, here at The SEED, lives are being changed every day! But this is only possible through the generosity of friends like you.

For those that cannot thank-you themselves, let me assure you of their heartfelt gratitude for this wonderful gift of new life."

I know it was not a whole lot of money, but who couldn't feel motivated and inspired after receiving a letter like this?

What a great day for me. And the great news continued.

ENERGIZED

Billy Batdorf phoned back (letting me know that Connie had asked him to phone back), and this time we talked for over an hour. He had matched the $100 Connie had sent with $100 of his money and then donated it to an organization called KIVA (www.kiva.org). KIVA is a micro-lending organization that helps business people in underdeveloped and third world countries. Kiva 'connects people through lending to alleviate poverty' and Kiva is all about 'Loans that change Lives'. Guess where Billy's donation went to? Yes, a lady in Costa

Rica who needed to expand her restaurant because she provided lunches for her whole village.

Billy said that, since the donation was in my name, I should have received via email, all of the website information and the thank-you from KIVA. The business lady in Costa Rica has since paid the loan back and we agreed to leave the money with KIVA for more loans. Billy has since contributed more money. Just the other day he shared with me via email that all of the money he has donated, including the original "Pay It Forward 10" $100, is now in 7 loans to 7 business people in a number of different countries. Very cool.

I called Connie to thank her for what she had done and asked how many people she had done this with. She wouldn't say.

The next week, a cheque for $1,000 from Andrew arrived in the mail. We started a search for a local athlete in need and utilized a few of the local Lethbridge sports media to help.

INSPIRATION FROM THE EAST

Soon after, I was just about to get out of my van to go in for a haircut (yes, it is true. I still need haircuts even though most of the work required is on the sides now instead of on the top), when I received a call on my cell from Wadey. Wade Lyon is my cousin. We were born about a month apart and grew up together in Barons, Alberta, Canada, Paradise. We went through 12 years of regular school together, followed by two years of Telecommunications Technology at the Southern Alberta Institute of Technology in Calgary. After graduation, Wadey took a job with Northern Telecom in Ottawa, Ontario and I stayed in Alberta with Alberta Government Telephones (now Telus). So we went from seeing each other almost daily to seeing each other once in a blue moon – when Wadey came west to visit family and friends. Wadey is incredibly smart, a great friend and, as you may remember from an earlier Chapter, he became the star of the "in-town" football team at recess. Plus, Wadey was the one that saved me during the dead battery, dressed only in a diaper fiasco after Halloween. That is perhaps the best way to describe Wadey. He gives people a boost.

Wadey shared with me that he too had received $100 from Connie. Wadey and his wife Lynn matched it and donated to the Children's Hospital of Eastern Ontario in Ottawa (www.cheo.on.ca). Two of their children had spent time at the hospital. I received a package of information in the mail about the Children's Hospital with a thank-you note from another wonderful "worthy cause". I think the best part was Wadey's and Lynn's letter to me. A couple of excerpts from that letter are below:

"CHEO is a world-class facility dedicated to the care and well being of youth 18 years of age and under. All of the kids are amazing! No matter how sick they are or how terrible the prognosis is, the kids seem to be happy. The strength and the will demonstrated by these young people is simply inspiring. And that is due in no small part to the philosophy of CHEO and all of the fantastic people who work and volunteer there."

In the spring of 2009, I had the privilege to thank both Wadey and Lynn in person when my son Tommy was playing in the National Volleyball Championships in Ottawa. What great people the two of them are.

Kat, Billy, Andrew and Wadey so far. This was amazing stuff. My head was spinning and my energy level was through the roof.

INFLUENCE AND POTENTIAL AT EVERY TURN

Back to the $1,000 Andrew had mailed to me. Unable to find a needy athlete, the Inner Circle group was starting to put pressure on me to do something with the money. At our next quarterly retreat, two outstanding things happened. One, Andrew gave me a copy of Craig and Marc Kielburger's book "Me to We". The Kielburger's are founders of Free the Children (www.freethechildren.com) and the book "Me to We" is a must read for anyone and everyone. Don't think twice. Just go to www.amazon.com or www.chapters.indigo.ca and get it.

The other outstanding news I received at that quarterly retreat was that my Success Partner, Todd Guy, had also received a $100 bill from Connie. Todd is an incredibly successful businessman and has been helping me expand my comfort zone for over 5 years now. We talk by phone most Monday mornings. I attribute much of my business success and the increase in the value of our business to Todd's mentoring, inspiration, leadership, and kicks in the ass. Todd shared that he had donated the money to the national charity for The UPS Store in Canada, the Tuppy's Children Foundation, because of my long relationship with The UPS Store. Tuppy's provided monies to economically challenged families who have a challenged child. They needed items such as wheelchairs, lifts, bathroom adaptations or expansions, special beds, etc. – anything that was immediately necessary to make life easier for both child and parents. The stories that came from head office were extremely heart warming.

Todd was "Pay it Forward" number five that I knew about and I left our Inner Circle retreat on cloud 9 and with the book "Me to We" under my arm.

I am away from home a lot on business. One thing I used to enjoy when the kids were smaller was them all piling in our bed so that I could read or tell a story to them. Even though they were well past the age of having stories read to them, when I came home with the book "Me to We", I convinced them to once again pile into our bed for a number of evenings. Until we read that book together, we did not know who Craig and Marc Kielburger were or what "Free the Children" was all about. What a great story. I am serious when I say that you need to get a copy of this book. The kids searched online to discover even more about this remarkable organization. Now we knew why Andrew gave us this book and it was clear where the $1,000 needed to go.

Our children, Tommy, Davey and Maggie made the final decision. Since we had lived in Thailand for 4 years and both Davey and Maggie were born there, the kids chose Free the Children's micro-credit and business training/resources program for women in Southeast Asia. Inspired by Connie's $100, expanded by Andrew Barber-Starkey and the

Inner Circle, and directed by my children, it is very special knowing that many women will be able to grow their businesses, grow their business knowledge, and help their communities and families.

 ### DANNY DIAMOND SUCCESS TIP:
The act of giving escalates from fantastic to ultra-fantastic when you involve your kids and the whole family.

DEAN MARTIN TIME

Connie read somewhere a long time ago that no matter what was going on in Dean Martin's professional life, when his kids were small his wife insisted that all rehearsing and shooting stop so that they could have dinner together as a family at 6 pm. Since I am on the road a lot, making it difficult to be home every night at 6 pm, Connie and I agreed that I would do everything possible to make it home by 6 pm on Friday evenings. We called it *Dean Martin Time*.

Connie called one week and told me I had to be home by Dean Martin Time on Friday evening and to not plan anything else. I did as instructed. Three special guests arrived.

Bernie Johnston is the mother of Taylor, who has played soccer with our son Tommy since the boys were 8 or 9 years old. Bernie is a nurse by profession, which makes her a natural "giver". And Givers Gain.

The other two special guests were Robbie and Lynn Cowie from Nanton, Alberta. Robbie and I grew up together in Barons. The last 9 or 10 years we have been going fishing in the mountains, just as we did when we were kids. Although not nearly as keen on fishing as I once was (I now more enjoy having a beer while "guarding" the campfire and testing out how comfortable the camp chairs are.), the time away with no laptop and no cellular coverage is extremely valuable and revitalizing. Despite all of my travels throughout the world, I have yet to find a better holiday place than a secluded area in the mountains and I am very pleased that my children love it up there as well. Part of their "loving it" is because Robbie has taught all of my kids how to fly fish. Both Robbie and Lynn are teachers and natural givers. And Givers Gain.

Bernie told her story first. Giving up holiday time and covering her own travel expenses, she had travelled to Quito, Ecuador with a surgical team from Edmonton called Canadian Association of Medical Teams Abroad (www.CAMTA.com). Her team was there for 10 days performing hip replacements in adults and club feet and other hip problems in infants and children for the underprivileged people of Quito and the surrounding area. Bernie shared with us that she was not concerned at all about utilizing the $100 Connie had provided to her as she thought she would simply pay for someone's hip operation – until the facilitators explained otherwise. The patients have to pay for their own surgery, anywhere from $5 to $200 depending on their income level, as it is felt that if they have to pay they will be more accountable for their health.

As is true with most things in life, there is more value, more accountability in having to pay for something – whether that payment is in time or money.

Bernie shared that she got nervous, as her time in Ecuador grew short and she still had not come up with a viable way to donate the money. She talked to one of the social workers and it was decided to spend the money on 22 year old Daniel, who the team had performed surgery on earlier in the week because of an infected hip. Daniel Vega Moreno is the 8th of nine children and had a total of four surgeries on both hips by the time he was 5 years old. After a fairly normal childhood, Daniel had gone through a serious of complications over the last few years with his hips that severely challenged the family economically. This culminated in chronic infection and the need for the surgery performed while Bernie was in Ecuador. Daniel would now require long term antibiotics, physiotherapy and numerous doctor visits which would be over and above the cost of the surgery. Bernie said she was very excited to do this for Daniel but, she questioned, would $100 be enough? While in

Ecuador and relating the story of how she obtained the $100, Bernie said many of the medical personnel on her team were excited to contribute. As well, when she returned to Canada, Bernie contacted CAMTA and received all of the information on Daniel; then both Bernie and her sister contributed enough money to ensure that the total amount needed was reached. In Bernie's letter to me she said

"Thank-you to you and your lovely wife Connie for giving me this opportunity to fulfill this 50th birthday present to you. It was a very gratifying experience for me. I hope you have a happy 50th year and many more birthdays to celebrate."

Bernie gave me information on all they had done in Ecuador, plus the amazing story of Daniel and pictures of Bernie at Daniel's bedside in Quito. The real thanks, of course, goes to Bernie, an incredible woman and "giver", and all that she does for people in the world.

Robbie and Lynn's story was emotional as well. In two separate, tragic accidents, a Junior High student and a High School Student from the small community of Nanton, Alberta had been killed. Memorial Scholarship funds were established in their honour – The Logan Burnett Memorial Scholarship Fund (Junior High) and The Greg Dawson Memorial Scholarship Fund (High School). Since Robbie and Lynn's children had benefitted from the Greg Dawson Memorial Scholarship, and since they were both long time teachers in Nanton, they made the decision that these scholarship funds were where the money for my 50th needed to go. Robbie and Lynn matched the $100 Connie had provided with $100 of their own.

That is not where the story ends. During this time, a local rancher had provided Robbie and Lynn with tickets to a Calgary Flames hockey game. When the rancher refused to accept payment for these tickets, the Cowies took the money they had offered for the hockey tickets and added it to the total towards the scholarships. Each of the Scholarship Funds received $250. Robbie wrote great letters of explanation to the Trustees of both funds, ensuring that the local rancher who had provided the hockey tickets was recognized. We later received very inspiring and moving letters back from the Scholarships, as well as a thank-you note to Robbie and Lynn from the grandmother of one of the boys.

Robbie and Lynn have dedicated their lives to helping others and perhaps the excerpt from the Greg Dawson Memorial Scholarship fund letter below says it best about Robbie and Lynn, as well as what Connie initiated with the "Pay It Forward 10".

"The Cowies were among those who initiated the fund after Greg's death. You have chosen well by including them in your birthday giving list. Rob shared your story and method of celebrating an important milestone with me and offered the Greg Dawson Memorial Scholarship Fund a generous donation to mark that occasion. Rob and Lynn have contributed much of their professional careers to the Nanton schools and their efforts have not gone unnoticed by those of us lucky to have had kids under their care and guidance throughout their education. Please accept our thanks for your generosity and for choosing the Cowies to "pay it forward". Our committee was impressed by your initiative and the way you celebrated such a milestone. It really was a "feel good" story that could teach us all something about giving."

COFFEE BREAK

Every so often I am lucky enough to be in Lethbridge on a Friday morning and can meet at the Southside Tim Hortons coffee shop to visit with some of my former Alberta Government Telephones and Telus colleagues. They bring back great memories and help me stay grounded with Lethbridge and what is happening in town. Sometimes, Ron Hillmer is able to make it to these Friday morning coffee sessions. Ronny and I started working together in 1976, and this extended to travels working together in the U.S. and Thailand. Ronny was a huge support in a tough stretch for me in the late 80's and was the best man at Connie's and my wedding in 1990. When Ronny returned from Thailand, he brought with him his beautiful wife Warin (pronounced Wa-Lynn), who did nothing but improve Ronny's life in every area and we are so glad they found each other.

At one of the coffee mornings with "the boys", months after my birthday, I was explaining some of what you have already read. That is when the light bulb went on for Ronny and he announced that he was supposed to give me a call. He too was one of the "Pay it forward" group. Ronny explained that he and Warin wanted to do something for the kids in Thailand because, she was from there, plus all of us (meaning Ronny, Connie and I, and the kids) had lived there. Through Warin's sister, they found a school for disadvantaged and distressed children in the rural area a few hours north of Bangkok near Phitsanulok. The very next week, Ronny and I were able to meet for coffee again and he brought with him the information from Thailand, including a letter from the head teacher and pictures of the kids at assembly.

Wat Photiyan School was a former temple converted to a school with around 100 students who, as per the description of the school's head teacher, were *"children from broken homes, children discarded by parents, orphans, and poor children from the minority groups among the hill tribes."* And like many of these institutions that are formed simply because of the need, the head teacher went on to say that the little help they receive from the Government is "not enough for these children to survive and get an education." Again, working with and through Warin's sister, it was determined that the school had upkeep and renovation challenges. One of the biggest issues was that there was no girl's bathroom. This became the project that Ronny and Warin tackled. They matched the money Connie had provided and, I am pretty sure, added more to that amount to ensure that a new bathroom was built. Ronny said it was quite a process, a lot of leg work by Ronny, Warin and Warin's sister and a lot of correspondence to ensure that the money was indeed dedicated to the bathroom. As with all of the pay it forward contributions and projects, what an outstanding way for my 50th birthday and the giving of the "Pay It Forward 10" to have some legacy. Ronny presented me with a thank-you letter from the school, in Thai writing, plus an update from his sister-in-law that the girls were so very happy that they no longer had to share the bathroom with the boys. Another "extra" effort of giving and my hat is off to Ronny and Warin.

That made 8 people I knew of who had now shared their stories.

YOUR BROTHER CALLED

The next call relating to the "Pay it Forward" group came from my older brother Bobby. A Captain with Air Canada Airlines, Bobby moved away from home right out of high school to get his pilot's license and has been flying ever since. I was always impressed that he knew what he wanted to do while still a teenager (and probably before that), then used discipline, dedication and determination to see it through and attain what he desired – a commercial pilot's license and a career with a large airlines.

He was calling for a couple of reasons. Bobby, my sister Penny, younger brother Jimmy and I contribute to the Vauxhall Academy of Baseball (www.vauxhallbaseball.com) in the name of our grandfather, Alvan Lyon. Bobby called to say his share was on its way. Officially, we donate $1,000 annually to the Alvan Drew Lyon Bursary. My grandfather loved baseball and drove us to just about every little league game any of us ever played. We thought it appropriate to provide a legacy to him, especially when such a special academy was established in a smaller community, much like we all came from.

The second reason Bobby called was to explain what he had done with the $100 Connie has sent to him. Aha! #9 of the "Pay it forward" group. Bobby wanted to make the contribution sports related while helping those who would maximize the use of the money. He chose the Special Olympics and, because of my love for baseball, Bobby asked them to direct it to the youth baseball team. I hope they were able to do that. That very day, I swear it's true, I received a thank-you note in the mail from Special Olympics that read:

A generous contribution has been made in honour of
Mr. Danny Lyon
to Special Olympics by
Mr. Robert Lyon

"This gift will help us continue to touch more lives and make
it possible for a greater number of children with intellectual
disabilities to experience the joy of competition and participate
in the sharing of gifts, skills and friendships.

EXTREMELY IMPRESSIONABLE

As I write about all that transpired above, and re-read the excellent letters and thank-you notes from the charities, schools, scholarship funds, patients, etc., who received this money, I get all jazzed up and inspired once again. And it wasn't over.

My sister-in-law Kathy and her daughter Katie came down to Lethbridge to visit and see Kathy's older daughter Breanne, who was attending Lethbridge College. Although family, Kathy is Connie's and my business partner with The UPS Store and heads up all operations and training to do with the Franchise in our Area. Kathy is a success story in and of herself, as a single mother of two daughters. She invested everything she had in the business more than 11 years ago, when she had never been in business before. Talk about moving out of one's comfort zone! Kathy is a "can-doer", a roll up her sleeves and get after the task kind of person. Willing to do anything to help the Franchisees become more successful, Kathy is extremely well respected and is an integral part of the success of our business.

#10 of the "Pay it forward" group was exposed when Kathy shared with me what she had done with the $100 Connie had given to her.

Several weeks after my 50th birthday, we were on The UPS Store Canada national convention cruise in the Caribbean. On that trip, Kathy explained to a number of people what Connie had done and many wanted to be a part of it. How they all kept it secret from me I don't know.

Eighteen people from across the network, meaning across the country, helped get the total up to $1,100 and that is what Kathy presented to me - along with the responsibility of donating it to an appropriate cause.

As the "Pay it Forward 10" stories came out and I shared them with other people, Connie and I started hearing stories on a weekly basis from people who had been touched and took it upon themselves to do something similar. In addition, we heard from the "Pay it Forward" group and the people they had involved or touched that the "giving" was continuing and many people had been inspired to do more. With this in mind, I made a decision on the $1,100 that Kathy had raised. I donated $600 of it to the local Lethbridge Chapter of Big Brothers and Big Sisters. I also provided $100 each to what I considered 5 influential people in the Lethbridge Area along with a detailed description of what had transpired to date, all with the desire to keep the chain going for as long and in as much of an extended capacity as possible. Unfortunately, I never received a response from Big Brothers and Big Sisters of any kind, and only three of the five receiving the $100 got back to me on what they did with the money. What I do know in my heart is that the money was well received and that the 5 donated to extremely worthy causes.

These are great people mentioned throughout this Chapter and I believe what Connie and all of these people did can be summed up in my paraphrased version of a letter I received from a local politician:

'They are all to be congratulated for their altruistic actions. I'm certain that they are wonderful parents, friends, associates and leaders and have given others a strong background with which to be fine citizens. I would expect that the kind of generosity exemplified will live in their memories and the memories of those they have touched, and perhaps colour choices and enhance opportunities for the rest of their lifetimes. No doubt friends and acquaintances have been affected and I congratulate them for making their communities an even better place for all to call home.'

HOW DO YOU TOP IT?

The "Pay it forward 10" and those they involved touched thousands of people's lives. How does one top what Connie started and all that these great people accomplished? Neither Connie nor I had an answer.

In October, 2007, Connie, Tommy, Davey, Maggie and I were on the Bob Proctor Cruise to the Mexican Rivera. It was a fantastic experience and we signed up for the October, 2008 Bob Proctor Cruise, this time to the Caribbean, as soon as it was announced. Bob Proctor is one of the gurus of personal development, as well as one of the stars of the movie "The Secret". If you have never seen him live, you must (www.bobproctor.com).

On the cruises, Bob provided some of the top speakers and teachers on success and personal development including Gerry Robert, Mark Victor Hansen, Rev. Michael Beckwith, Mary Morissey, Steven Siebold, Debbie Ford, Peggy McColl, and Paul Martinelli, to name a few. It is one thing to see great speakers live, and it is extra special to be in an intimate setting with them for several days. The cruises were outstanding.

Sitting in the audience before one of the sessions on the October, 2008 cruise, Connie and I were discussing what we should do for my 51st birthday to keep the momentum going from what she and the "Pay it forward 10" had created for my 50th. Our conversation was interrupted by the next speaker on stage, Cynthia Kersey, the bestselling author of "Unstoppable" and "Unstoppable Women". These are two more books that should be in everyone's library. A dynamic speaker, Cynthia was sharing what her foundation (www.unstoppable.net) had been doing to build housing and schools in Asia and Africa. She explained that for her birthday she invited as many in her network as possible to her party and in lieu of birthday gifts, asked them to donate for the purpose of building a school in Africa. Along with a live auction and silent auction, Cynthia said it was a huge success.

As Cynthia finished her presentation, Connie and I almost spoke at the same time. That was it! A birthday party for my 51st birthday where Connie and I provided and paid for the venue, the band and the food, and we invited our whole network to attend. Connie asked me if I could have any band play at my birthday party, who would it be? I said The Chevelles, one the best cover bands I have ever seen in all of my travels and whose members just happen to live in Lethbridge. Connie then asked me where we would hold the birthday bash. I said one of the best places in town is the D.A. Electric Barn at Lethbridge College because it is set-up for the exact kind of party we were contemplating.

Later, I ran into Cynthia in the hallway of the cruise ship and I told her how she had inspired us and that we were going to "borrow" her idea for my birthday. I wanted to know more about the Unstoppable Giving Challenge she had established to raise money for schools in Africa. When she shared with me that she had partnered with Free the Children to build the schools and that 100% of the money raised went to this purpose, I was in. Cynthia also explained that the website was just about ready to launch after the cruise and if I wanted to be one of the test sites, I was welcome. I accepted.

GET WITH IT, MAN.

Upon returning from the cruise, I must admit I did not do much about the proposed birthday bash and fundraiser for about two weeks, even though it was now November and my birthday was on January 19th. All I had to do was "expose" our plans to our network and their support and motivation got the "Danny Diamond is Almost 51 Years Old and Unstoppable Giving Challenge Celebration" moving full speed ahead.

- The bass guitar player for The Chevelles is a courier driver. While dropping off a package at our house, I explained what we were planning and, although they were booked 18 months in advance, there were sometimes cancellations. He provided the business card for band's drummer, Don, who handles all of the bookings.

- Don had a cancellation just that morning for January 10th. Talk about luck. "Do you want it?" Don asked. The answer was yes and I immediately drove a deposit cheque over to his office. The Chevelles preferred venue? The same as mine - the D.A. Electric Barn.

- I called the Lethbridge College and tracked down the person responsible for the Barn's bookings. "Yes", it was available on January 10th. Another deposit cheque was delivered.

- A good friend suggested a caterer and they too were available for January 10th.

- The UPS Store did up promotional postcards, posters and tickets for the event.

- We handed out the postcards at our kid's volleyball and soccer games. So many people helped us spread the word very quickly.

- Cynthia Kersey's office contacted me to announce that my website was up and working. Anyone donating $100 or more at my (or anyone's) Unstoppable Giving Challenge website, would also receive the Million Dollar Idea program - success lessons from Cynthia's network of top success and personal development leaders.

- I blasted an email to my whole database explaining the "Pay it forward 10"; the birthday bash and building a school in Africa; and with the website address Cynthia's team had established for us. Anyone donating $100 or more received two free tickets to the birthday bash.

MOTIVATE THE MOTIVATOR

What a great response we received.

- People from across Canada, the U.S. and even from Thailand donated at the site.

- Tickets sales were brisk.

- Several groups wanted tables for 8.

- I stopped in to see friend Vicky Miller, who owned a liquor store in town, and she asked to take over everything to do with the bar for the event.

- People were contacted about the silent auction and donations were abundant.

- Also, People called us to donate to the silent auction.
- Friend Sue Manery pretty much organized and set up the whole silent auction with help from Connie and several soccer moms.
- Local radio and TV personality, Mark Campbell, agreed to emcee the event.
- Retired auctioneer Keith Erdmann agreed to attend as my guest and handle the live auction items.
- My niece Breanne, who was in the Criminal Justice program at Lethbridge College, organized a number of classmates to volunteer to take tickets at the door, handle silent auction cash and reconciliation, do the coat check, handle the bar ticket sales and, most importantly, provide rides home to anyone that needed a ride.
- Most of my Inner Circle mastermind group was able to attend.
- Most of the "Pay it Forward 10" were able to attend.
- Cynthia shipped a video of her work in Africa that we showed on a loop during the evening.
- Even before the big evening got under way, we had raised over $10,000 U.S.

The big day finally arrived.

- While setting up at the D.A. Electric Barn, I received a call from Cynthia Kersey and she provided an excellent introduction and welcome for everyone on my voicemail.
- The band's roadies came early to set up.
- The UPS Store and my niece Breanne worked throughout the day to provide sponsor notices on each table as well as individual sponsor cards and bid sheets for each silent auction item.
- The caterers had everything set up well in advance.

- We were still setting up the silent auction area with the help of a group of some very wonderful ladies when guests started arriving. Even though I still needed to get home for a shower and shave, several of gthe guests told me that we should make this an annual event. The evening had not even started and there was talk of an annual event!

ENERGIZED EVENING.

In all, about 170 people sat down for dinner and 35 more came for the dance. Cynthia's welcome was excellent as we plugged my Blackberry and her voicemail into the sound system. Mark Campbell was fantastic as MC and Keith Erdmann did an outstanding job with the live auction, even auctioning off the right to be the first table through the buffet. Although they did not know that they had to, the "Pay it Forward 10" in attendance were asked to come up on stage and share their stories. It was very powerful once again. Everyone said the meal was great and that the roast beef was some of the best they had ever had. The Chevelles then rocked the place until 1 am or 2 am or whatever it was. The bar did well, the silent auction was more than I ever expected, and the Criminal Justice students drove a bunch of people home. What a success the event turned out to be.

When the smoke cleared, the total for the evening was about another $10,000 U.S. making our total raised to that date about $20,000. Additional donations came in over the next few weeks, including funds raised by several kindergarten, elementary and middle schools in Lethbridge and Area.

After spending a month $3,500 U.S. short of our goal of $25,000 to build a school, another email update was provided. I immediately received a reply from business partner and mentor Mr. Ralph Askar, a great man and who had already donated to the cause earlier. Ralph said that if I was able to raise $1,750, he would personally match it and the goal would be reached. When the next email went out to everyone with Ralph's challenge, the money was raised in a very short time, Ralph matched it as promised, and there was carry over such that the very final total was $26,004 U.S.

We did it!

What great support from such great people – and all for the kids of Kenya.

LIMITLESS POSSIBILITIES

In one of my update conversations with Cynthia, I explained that I was in a web based business with my 15 year old son Davey. He was so inspired by the fundraising for the kids in Africa that he wanted to create another business account and donate the proceeds to the schools. A few days later Cynthia called to invite both Davey and I on the trip she was organizing to Kenya in July. We immediately accepted.

In July, 2009, Davey and I formed part of Cynthia's Unstoppable group to Kenya and spent 7 days on the Maasai Mara through Free the Children. It was fantastic. We visited the villages and the schools everyday and learned firsthand the great work Free the Children does through their Adopt a Village program. We got to work on a classroom and were able to attend the grand opening of a classroom that was built with funds that had been raised by our group.

No electricity, no clean water, most people without shoes, limited clothing plus all of the challenges of 3 years of drought, plus aids and other diseases – yet the people of the Maasai Mara were the happiest I had ever met. They were incredible, amazing and ultra-fantastic all rolled into one.

We tagged on a couple of days for another lifelong dream of mine, a Safari in Africa. When we left for Africa, Davey, like me, thought the safari would be a highlight. However, after spending time with the people of the Maasai Mara, both Davey and I agreed that the Safari, although great, was anti-climatic and we would have rather spent two more days at the schools and in the villages.

Upon returning to Nairobi, we were treated with a very great bonus. Craig Kielburger, the founder of Free the Children, met us at the Wilson Airport and took almost two hours out of his very busy schedule to be with us. Incredible!

I can't thank Cynthia enough for inviting us to Kenya. I know it was her influence that got us extra tours of schools and I know it was her presence that caused Mr. Kielburger to spend time with us.

WE DAY

After we returned to Canada, I received two extremely important emails. One was from Cynthia saying that she had attained two VIP tickets to Free the Children's "We Day" in Vancouver that was headlined by the Dalai Lama. One ticket was for me and one was for Davey. I could not attend unfortunately and Connie felt it was important that the kids go. Tommy and Maggie decided between themselves and Maggie was chosen. Then, the second email came from Craig Kielburger, and he provided another VIP ticket which meant Tommy could go as well.

On September 29th, 2009 Tommy (17), Davey (now 16), and Maggie (13) travelled to We Day Vancouver to meet up with Cynthia Kersey and see a speaking line-up that included musician Jason Mraz, Craig Kielburger, Jane Goodall, Mia Farrow, Marc Kielburger, child soldier Michel Chikwanine, motivational speaker Spencer West, entrepreneur and activist Brett Wilson, and, of course, the Dalai Lama. What a great experience for young people, including the Lyon kids. When I asked Tommy if it was worth missing volleyball for, he didn't just say yes, he said "definitely yes". They all want to go back next year.

It doesn't stop there.

While we were in Africa, Davey and I noticed that the country was soccer crazy, yet we only saw one homemade soccer ball at all of the schools we visited. Made from plastic bags and twine, it was about the size of a softball.

The grade 8 boys at Emorijoi School guarded the ball. I asked them why there was only one. They said it was because of the scarcity of plastic bags and the amount of time it took to make even a small ball like the one they had.

I had previously discussed with Free the Children facilitators about what, if anything, we could do concerning the lack of shoes, clothing, and school uniforms. They said that what we were doing through Cynthia's Unstoppable Foundation was probably the best for those things. However, when I inquired about providing soccer balls, the idea was welcomed by both the facilitators and the head teacher.

Therefore, we started a soccer ball drive and many amazing people across the great Province of Alberta have provided over 450 soccer balls to date; plus air pumps, uniforms, goalie equipment and even cleats. In addition, over $300 cash has been raised to help with shipping costs. Outstanding! I will always be amazed how giving people are and how so many just rise to the occasion whenever asked. We have started the process of getting everything to the Free the Children offices in Toronto so that they take it to Kenya. I am very much looking forward to pictures and video from the Maasai Mara of the kids playing with their new soccer balls and equipment – for years to come.

February 27th, 2010 is the next birthday event, as we attempt to make it an annual event. This time it is the "Danny Diamond is Over 52 Years Old and Unstoppable Foundation Celebration". The guest of honour will be Cynthia Kersey herself. Very special, as Cynthia is living proof that Givers Gain and that the giving never stops. I think it was Oprah Winfrey who said something along the lines of, 'a person never stops giving and giving is more than being able to write a cheque. It is the ability to touch other people's lives.' I believe that describes Cynthia Kersey, the "Pay it Forward 10", Connie Lyon, and everyone everywhere who helped us raise money and collect soccer balls. You have all touched so many other people's lives and I know the giving will continue. Givers Gain.

LIVING MARVELLOUSLY

As we move forward, the incredible inspiration I have received continues and the opportunities to spread out further and do even more are countless.

Amazingly, the opportunities in our business seem to correspond directly to the opportunities to give. What we give in time, money and effort seems to come back to us many times over.

I mentioned earlier that if you want to be more prosperous, more successful – both monetarily and in your soul – then give, without expecting anything in return. The less you think you *have* to give is the perfect time *to* give. Prosperity through giving comes in many forms such as increased income, good health, good ideas, guidance, mentoring and, perhaps the best of all, satisfaction and inner peace – becoming rich spiritually, emotionally and mentally.

 DANNY DIAMOND SUCCESS TIP:
Give to energize, inspire and motivate yourself.
Give to energize, inspire and motivate others around you.
"If it is going to be, it is up to me."

Each day is made up as we go along. The best part is we get to choose at each minute along the way how and if we will act, how and if we will *respond*, whether we will lead the way or follow, and what emotions we will allow to take over.

The world, *your world*, is a stage and you are on it, front and centre. Roll out your own red carpet. Show off your red carpet appeal by being the leader in giving of yourself whole heartedly.

Show off your potential, your confidence, your influence, your energy, your ability by giving it all you have with extreme vitality. Give to others as much of your time, your knowledge, your experience, your expertise, and, yes, even your money, at every appropriate opportunity.

This will build your network with a solid foundation and will expand it exponentially to its fullest potential.

People will be attracted to all of your positive qualities, especially your willingness to **Expose Yourself For Success** and give without expectations of return. You will help people reach their potential. You will help others make 180 degree turns in their lives for the better. You will motivate and create confidence. You will make yourself and others realize that the possibilities of success are *limitless*. While you continue to give away motivation, inspiration, knowledge, expertise, etc., what you get in return will continue to skyrocket you to more success.

Every other Chapter included an exercise to do at the end. There is no exercise at the end of this Chapter. Just a request.

"If it is going to be, it is up to me."

You know your desires and you're potential. Make it happen.

Live on purpose because you have the choice. There are only limitless possibilities. Seize them, grab them, and continue to always "go for it".

Help and give. Then help and give some more.

Do all the good you can
By all the means you can
In all the ways you can
In all the places you can
To all the people you can
As long as ever you can

—John Wesley

Impress yourself daily and live marvellously!

CHAPTER 10:

– Success Defined –

Success is the ability to go from one failure to
another with no loss of enthusiasm.

—Sir Winston Churchill

"Because we are all individuals, the "description/definition of success" varies for each of us. Even within ourselves, success can be defined relative to a particular moment or circumstance. Months ago, my lawyer was at my hospital bedside taking my will. When I took stock of the assets that I had left for my daughter, the feeling was "is that all?" I felt ordinary, even inadequate. On the other hand, I had no doubt of the love that my daughter had for me. The feeling was "I have been a good daddy".

So "success" for me is a feeling. A feeling of having made a difference for the better. The feeling is relative to a particular moment or circumstance which need not be generally perceived as a "great deed" or newsworthy. The action can be small but the feeling of having made a difference can be immense. This feeling is cumulative. When it's all said and done, and we know and feel that we have made a difference - that's the feeling of "success". Drink Tea and be well.

—Andrew Kang, Entrepreneur and Owner of
Elixir Fine Tea, www.elixirfinetea.com

"Success is a strict personal issue. It should not be compared or evaluated. It is the journey to your predetermined goal.

You have just to define what you really want to do. Not what other people want you to do. Follow your dreams and stay on course. This beautiful trip is your success."

—Xavier Debaere, Entrepreneur - Professional Speaker,
Comines, Belgium, www.xavierdebaere.com

"For us, Success is being able to live our lives with our careers, recreation, healthy lifestyle, personal relationships and personal growth in a comfortable balance. We believe that the mark of true Success is being fully at peace with oneself, one's family and one's friends."

- John & June Breeze - Citizens of the World and proud to be Canadians

"The bottom line is that if you become a master at handling problems and overcoming obstacles, what can stop you from success? The answer is nothing! And if nothing can stop you, you become unstoppable!"

—T. Harv Eker, Author of #1 NY Times Bestseller
Secrets of the Millionaire Mind

I read once that "True success is being able to look at yourself in the mirror and feel proud of who you are". In the same vein I feel that individual success is having the opportunity to live long enough to realize what your life is all about, and embracing that which is truly important.

—H.R. Beswick, Q.C.

Success is something very different to me – something that represents the accumulation of many daily victories to achieve an important, long-term goal. Sometimes success is re-defined as it is achieved, as the results exceed one's expectations.

I consider success to be many things including life's important milestones – earning a college degree, getting married to the right partner, having children, buying a house. These are many of the things that most people consider to be some of life's greatest accomplishments.

Other success is much more personalized. For me, success has also included living, traveling and working internationally, releasing an album of my own music, and earning an advanced degree in business. Each of these events I consider as personal successes; but in achieving them, I have found new goals and new opportunities for success. One success leads to another…like reaching a mountaintop and finding even higher mountains beyond.

—Ted Price, Manager, Special Venues Development,
Mail Boxes Etc./The UPS Store

My success definition: to do it yourself first. To prove to yourself you know how to achieve your goals. Then you have the ability to share. Teach others how to attain what you have. You are not successful until you are rich in all aspects of life. (Spiritual, Personal, Financially, generously gifting)

- Todd Guy, President, Independent Electric & Controls Ltd.,
www.iecgroup.ca

Success: You need 20 "no's to get a "yes". Stick with it. Get angry with people who get you down. Pessimism is the devil. Look around at just how successful you are. You are luckier than you think! Help someone get ahead. When they thank you, tell them, "Now go help someone else. That's the way it works". Don't allow yourself to get discouraged. Eat a bowl of rocky road ice cream and move on. Get on a road, any road. Even if it's the wrong road, that's ok. It's better than no road at all. Work with a mentor. If you don't have one, find one. Mentor someone (It feels good). Being bright is low on the list of success factors. Talk about your company or what you do with pride and enthusiasm. Listen more than you speak. Don't over react. Sometimes the solution takes time. Tenacity should be a virtue - oh ya it's called patience. Develop an attitude of "You know in your heart what is right. "Now just go do it".

—Barry Wilson, Director, National Account Manager,
Xerox Canada Ltd., www.xerox.com/index/enca.html

Success comes from within

It was October 1979 and I was the captain of the Canadian Hang Gliding Team at a competition in Chattanooga, Tennessee. It was a high-profile event and had attracted a large crowd. I was paired to compete head-to-head in a duration task against a top American pilot; the person who stayed up longest won. It was late in the day and there were no updrafts at all, so rather than being a test of pilot skill this event was primarily a test of hang glider performance. Unfortunately my opponent was flying a brand new prototype machine that gave him a significant performance advantage over my equipment. Everybody knew I was going to be badly beaten; the only question was by how much.

As I prepared myself to lose, I resolved to do everything I could to totally maximize the performance of my glider. That meant having a perfect takeoff, turning as little as possible, making my turns smooth and gentle, and landing on the bull's-eye.

As soon as we were in the air I realized my opponent was taking his equipment advantage for granted. He had a sloppy takeoff and was pretty much flying around aimlessly. My heart leapt. Maybe he would make a mistake and I would actually win.

My mind became focused and I was hyper-aware of everything around me. I flew my glider exactly at the perfect speed for maximum lift, never banking more than a few degrees throughout the entire flight. I tucked in my elbows and arched my back to reduce drag. It was like I was in an altered state; at one with my equipment and the fluid air that was providing lift for my flying machine.

Ten minutes later I glided in smoothly and made a perfect landing within a few feet of the bull's-eye. My opponent landed right behind me, beating me by a mere 20 seconds. The crowd went wild cheering his win, but both he and I knew his margin of victory should have been much,

much greater. And in that moment, I felt a level of success that has stayed with me ever since.

Why? After all, from an outsider's perspective I had lost the competition. Yet there was something inside telling me I had won.

I believe the reason so many people feel unsuccessful today is that society has conditioned us to measure our level of success by comparing ourselves to others. We have come to believe that success, is about impressing others -- having a beautiful body, an exotic car, a designer home or an expensive lifestyle. Preferably, all of the above. We are convinced that success means having lots of money even though the world is full of rich people who are very unhappy. We yearn for fame and recognition, thinking that acknowledgment from others will make us feel better about ourselves. None of these things are bad in their own right, but external validation can never make us feel successful; in fact sometimes the more recognition we get the more we feel like a fraud.

I have struggled greatly to feel successful in my own life. While hang gliding, I set numerous records, often flying higher and further than anyone else. I have a long list of credentials and achievements in the business and personal realms. Regrettably, far too many of these were motivated by my desire to impress others so they would notice me and tell me I was good enough.

In that hang gliding competition in 1979 I experienced success from within. I knew in my heart that I had given my best and felt proud of my effort and performance. I was at peace with myself. Unfortunately it was not until many years later that I realized feeling good about myself was the essential ingredient for true success.

Now, as an executive coach for entrepreneurs, I have the privilege of sharing what I've learned to assist my clients to have the experience of success by their own definition. In the process, I constantly learn more about myself and the feeling of fulfillment inside me continues to grow. Increasingly I'm able to look in the mirror and feel proud of myself, no matter what my external circumstances. To me, that is success.

—Andrew Barber-Starkey, Master Certified Coach,
The ProCoach Success System, www.ProCoachSystem.com

"Success is all about people, leadership and learning; it requires vision, integrity, presence of mind and dedication."

—Peter Salmon, Founder, Home-Alyze®, www.homealyze.com

"Success is coming to the point where you have the freedom to choose what to do at any given moment without worrying where the money will come from to pay the bills and still making a difference in the lives we touch.

Rolando and I, two 27 year old engineers, moved from Mexico in 2000 with just a bag of dreams but convinced that we would succeed in whatever enterprise we committed our hearts to.

In 2006, after working as employees for successful consulting companies, we decided to start our own Real Estate Investment Business. To do that we moved from Montreal to Edmonton where the market conditions were better. Now we own 45 rental properties and a 20 unit apartment building and, together, we are managing a growing General Contracting Business. We employ 7 people. And now even if the work days are long we feel closer and closer to our definition of success."

—Maribel Pecastre – President, Avant-Grade Properties Ltd.,
Edmonton, Alberta www.avant-garde-properties.com

In my life my greatest successes, the things that mean the most to me, have come when my actions have a positive impact that reaches beyond the original goal. Whether that has been hiring someone with talent but no experience and helping them flourish, or inspiring my team to achieve beyond what they thought was possible, I believe that success is shared glory and a feeling of accomplishment. From that comes earned respect, a sense of direction and purpose which, to me, is the very definition of success.

—Lorraine McLachlan, President & Chief Executive Officer,
Canadian Franchise Association, www.cfa.ca

For the longest time I believed success was something I did not possess. It was out of reach for me. I believed success was about money and status in life. My life has taken me on a journey I never expected and now I have more success than I ever dreamed possible. I now believe that success is a state of mind, it is the journey we take through life, it is the belief in yourself that anything is possible. Success is about setting your mind to something and doing anything and everything possible to achieve it. It is the desire to better yourself and help others in the process. When you can accept yourself and live the life you truly want, that is success. My son is going to grow up knowing anything can be achieved if you truly believe and that will be my biggest success of all.

—**Kari Berg, Live, Dream, Believe,** www.fhtmca.com/kberg

"A person's success in life belongs to them alone. Being able to get up in the morning and look in the mirror and like the man that's looking back at you is a measure of success. To look back at your life and think most of the things you set out to do, you did.

I am a Captain with a major airline and have been flying folks all over the world for over 35 years. Sometimes late at night on a long flight overseas, I will walk back into the cabin and see all the people that have put their trust in me to get them home safely. I am honoured that they trust me with their lives and for me, that simple trust is one of my biggest successes.

My wife and children are my rock. They have taught me more about living and life than anything else. They taught me what love and patience is and got me reacquainted with God."

—**Captain Robert Lyon, Air Canada**

To me success means that you are constantly improving, living life in the spirit of Kaizen. If you never settle, and are always looking for a way to make yourself better than you were yesterday, you are a success no matter what your current outside results might be.

—**Tammy Johnston: Founder and President of the Financial Guides,**
www.thefinancialguides.com

Success for me is to find peace. In order to find it, I need to harness all the energies at my disposal and through a medium of balanced mind and spirit, exercise my body and follow that path.

I was born in Kenya in 1954 when it was a British Colony.

I went to school to a 10th grade level in a town that had a swimming pool only at the hotel for tourists. I still do not swim. I ran the risk of being arrested by the government if I helped at my family's business. This was because I was of Indian heritage (foreign) with a British passport (colonial responsibility and therefore equally foreign) in an independent (1963) African country.

In 1971 I enrolled in a UK college with hard earned savings of my father after high school (grade 10). I studied full time until I was 21 to get my accounting designation.

In the meantime, I was threatened to be deported to Kenya if I sought employment to support myself because I was considered a 'foreign' student.

I eventually started my Accounting career in 1975 in the UK after successfully seeking permission to be a resident. I immigrated to Canada in 1982 and have three beautiful children one of whom got married in 2009. As a proud Canadian I enjoy the freedom and dignity that all life forms deserve. I have reached the maximum level (CFO) in my career. I started and have run a business for 15 years. By some accounts I may even be considered being in the top 5% of the world's population for comfort, security, etc.

By many standards, that IS success.

PS - I can now take swimming lessons...it is never too late.

—Mukesh Shah, CFO; Owner/Operator The UPS Store #74, Calgary, Canada; CEO Management 2000+, www.theupsstore.ca/74

Success is being of maximum service to others in the unique way that is authentically and only you. Of course, that requires that you take impeccable care of yourself in order to insure the capacity for maximum service.

—Phil Larson, RN, BSN, CCRN and Author of The-Anti-Diet, www.The-ANTI-Diet.com

Honesty, integrity, and humour in every aspect of my life and the rest will follow. Success is using the above principles to guide me while maintaining a strong vision and seeing that vision fulfilled. Always verify for yourself and do not stop until YOU are satisfied.

—Roger Morrison, Founder and Chairman of dtechs EPM, www.dtechs.ca

"For as long as I can remember I have always strived to be the most successful in everything I did. In other words, the top of the class in school, the best athlete and the best in business. As I grew older and wiser it was more important to me to experience the success that others enjoyed. I now rate myself successful when others achieve success; such as Franchisees coming into our business with nothing and achieving substantial monetary reward for hard work; parenting our children to be responsible parents and outstanding citizens. When others succeed because of your efforts, that accentuates success."

—Don Koenig, President & CEO,
Humpty's Restaurants International Inc., www.humptys.com

I was very fortunate to hear John Wooden speak on success very early on in my coaching career. His definition of success rang very true to me and I tried to base my coaching on it. John Wooden's definition of success states; "Success is peace of mind which is a direct result of self-satisfaction in knowing you made the effort to become the best that you are capable of becoming". This definition, along with the Pyramid of Success and it's building blocks that Coach Wooden designed became staples of my coaching practice. However, I had missed the point.

Despite believing that success isn't measured in wins and losses on the court, I was consumed with winning and trying to prove myself as a coach to my peers. My ultimate goal was to win the 4A high school boys provincial championship. Any season that did not deliver this goal, felt like a failure to me. The turning point came in the 2003 season. I had an amazingly talented team. I had a provincial team member in every position, plus two guys coming off the bench that were provincial team members...the dream team. As this season progressed, I knew that we were not really improving as players, and we certainly weren't coming anywhere close to "making the effort to become the best that we were capable of becoming". We were, however, winning all the time; cruising towards the much desired provincial championship. Of course, the lack of effort and the lack of improvement came to haunt us, as we didn't even make it out of our zone, losing to teams that we had soundly beaten all year long. I knew that I had failed my team as a coach. I had not lived up to the definition of success that I believed in, and instead had gotten blinded by winning.

As soon as we got back to our school, I returned to my office and took all of the medals, plaques, trophies, etc that I had collected over the years and put them into a box never to see the light of day again. It was at this time that I also read a book by Jim Thompson called Double Goal Coach. In it he clearly described what I had been doing. I had been "lured by the scoreboard" and forgot about the "mastery". In Jim's words, "Mastery means we are constantly getting better. We are not satisfied with being better than someone else. We want to be the best, the best that we can be." He also explained that focusing on mastery leads to decreased anxiety and increased self-confidence (which leads to athletes working harder and sticking to tasks longer). While focusing on the scoreboard actually led to an increase in anxiety and a decrease in confidence. He had described my team.

As the season wore on, my players (and I) had become so consumed with winning that we were more concerned about not winning then we were about not improving. The uncontrollable outcome on the scoreboard became our only focus. We became more tentative and timid in our play as the fear of losing made us more nervous, eventually resulting in us playing our worst volleyball of the season and losing out at zones. The dream team had become a nightmare!

As soon as we changed our focus from the scoreboard to mastery (and finally truly understanding Coach Wooden's definition) our program transformed. Winning became a by-product of success. Success itself was only achieved when we felt that we had lived up to Coach Wooden and Jim Thompson's definitions. We only worried about getting better and giving it our best effort each and every game and practice. Ironically our change in focus led to more success on the scoreboard as well. The program made four straight provincial finals (2006, 2007, 2008 and 2009) winning it all in 2007 with a 59-0 match record. Not once during that year was winning discussed. Effort, improvement and personal bests were all we strived for.

—Ard Biesheuvel, B.Ed and M.Ed; President, STARS Volleyball; Author; Head Coach Lethbridge Collegiate Institute Rams Volleyball; www. coachingvolleyballchampions.com

"A Small Measure of Success!"

When I took the leap of faith from regular pay check to the unknown world of being an entrepreneur, I learned many lessons along the way...

Now instead of having one boss, I had 50 bosses... they are called customers.

So called quitting time is no longer 5 pm... it is whenever the job is done.

I used to collect a pay check, now I have to go collect payment.

My small measure of success is having the option to go to a matinee movie on a Thursday afternoon.

I take small pleasure in knowing that I am sitting in a comfortable seat, in a nice cool theatre waiting for some action thriller to start while others frantically go about their day.

There is a sense of freedom and success having the choice to sit in a theatre almost alone enjoying hot buttered popcorn and a great flick.

My definition of success you ask?

"Think big thoughts... relish small pleasures."

—DJ Richoux, President, Business Breakthrough Technologies Inc.

In 1997 I was Mom to a six year old boy, my son Corey, and I was about to become a single Mom. At the same time, I also made the decision to leave the corporate world and become an entrepreneur. A car accident provided a divine message to think about what was truly important. Now when I look back at it, I ask myself what on earth I was thinking to believe that I could somehow pull of both of these monumental tasks. Somehow though I found the courage and I leaped!! Corey became my reason and my inspiration and my need to be his role model challenged me to become more and rise above my circumstances. At that time, I asked myself "what would success look like as a parent". When he was 18 or 20 or 22, how would I know if I had been successful in my role as his Mom.

I remember being impacted by a Jackie Kennedy quote that said something about how nothing else matters if we blow raising our children. As I thought about success as Corey's Mom, I decided that it meant two things to me. One was that he would have a solid foundation of faith and values from which to live his life. The other item on my success list was that he would have the understanding and the confidence to know that he is special and here to contribute something of value to the world. I knew that I needed to give him tools for his personal toolbox that would empower him to live his best life.

As I think about defining success as a parent 12 years ago and where we are today, I can definitely see the successful outcome of what I started when he was just a boy. By starting with the end in mind, my definition of success became the stand I took and the way I made decisions along the way. He's a young man now and I know I have given him a truly incredible start in life. He has roots and he has wings and I know I did well!!

—Sonja Skage, Real Estate Investor

Danny Lyon asked me to define success. I mulled it over, typed a few paragraphs and then hit delete. I typed a few more paragraphs and once again hit delete. I resolved to myself that I would not make a submission, because I wasn't sure or even worse, maybe I did not know the definition of success.

Then this morning as I was checking my email I noticed an email from Danny: "...improves the life of your customer..." was part of the quote he sent me from Paul Zane Pilzer. Then it hit me: Danny is successful, and "Why is that?" I asked myself. It's because everything he does, and everything he is, improves the life of everyone around him, including himself.

So although I can't take credit for it, I will gladly claim it as my own.

My definition of success can be summed up in this short sentence: "You are successful when, each day you live, everything you do improves the life of someone else and in turn improves your own."

—Jeff Parker, Owner The UPS Store #65
and The UPS Store #372, Alberta, Canada

Success is a heart function; it is not determined by the mind. For me, success is how I serve others: how I am attentive to the impact of my words and how I listen and hear what is said between the words.

I experience success moment by moment. To be present in the moment, I live in awareness of what is happening and I make conscious choices at each moment.

Success is all about me! It is totally dependent on me: my thoughts and my actions. Success is about 'the me' the person I take along wherever I go. At the end of the day, when I know I have done my best, that I have been present to every moment and I have lived at choice, I live in success.

—Lynn Thomson, Business Owner, Small Business Coach and Consultant

My definition of success is: Discovering my passion and purpose; honouring myself enough to do that for the rest of my life; living my life of Joy.

It seems to me that the greatest success comes when we are willing to step of the ledge, jump off the cliff, only see the next step…all of those wonderful truisms.

Success only comes with trusting, once you have made the 'leap', that even the scary days when you are living your passion and purpose with joy, are better than any days when you were doing what someone else wanted you to do; and becoming who someone else wanted you to become.

This life is only about Joy – of that I am certain – every minute, every hour and every day. When I discovered my Life Path, my passion and purpose – Joy and success has been the natural outcome.

—Dr. Debra Ford, Msc.D, www.LifeofJoy.ca

Success is not what you have in your bank account or how many toys you have. As a Business Owner in the Hospitality Industry it is … a satisfied customer. A customer who when asked how was their experience at your business smiles and replies to say anything positive! That to me is success… a team effort accomplishment that provided satisfaction to a customer(s).

Success in the Hospitality Industry is not the efforts of one person it is the team you work with whether it is providing excellent food, product, service or atmosphere but could also be a charity event in your establishment that brought the team together towards a goal for an individual or organization who needed the support, services or contributions. A SMILE on the face of a staff member or customer is the indication of success:)

—Vicky Miller, co-owner/operator,
Honkers Pub & Eatery Ltd., www.honkerspub.com

I find that success for me often starts as a fleeting thought, dreaming, having the courage to try despite possible failure, becoming passionate about the pursuit of whatever it is, and then making the dream a reality.

—Bernadette Johnston, RN

"All of the highly successful people that I have met have at some time in their lives, let go of their ego. This has a remarkable effect on the individual, allowing them to focus on profitable actions, the freedom to build strong teams around them and most importantly working in areas that they truly enjoy instead of areas that the ego demands of them. We have all met successful or famous people only to be surprised how down to earth they are, how easy they are to talk to. This to me is the true meaning of success."

—Rhett Thurston, Managing Director, MBE Australia and New Zealand

On Success…

I journey through life by creating goals and intentions. Once I reach these goals I celebrate, set a guidepost, and move on to the next ones. As I get older I now appreciate the new vista from which I can look back at the guideposts along my path of life, see them as successes and rejoice in their attainment.

—Cameron James, Director Of Operations
—Unity Telecom, www.unitytelecom.net

Success to me is when you have a goal and your main focus is on that goal against the obstacles that always arise. I have found through my life's experiences that if the goal is high, the time commitment and energy required to reach the goal is often 10 times of what I originally thought. Another key element in my life's successes is to find a coach/mentor who is excellent in the endeavour that is my goal. For example, I am a competitive paddler and wanted to compete in world class competitions. I sourced out a coach who was an Olympic paddler. This coach enlightened me to the techniques of paddling, the level of training and cross training that would be required and the thousands of hours of practice. I have competed in a number of world championships and have placed in the top three on two occasions for my age group.

—Gary Lokar, The UPS Store Area Franchisee for British Columbia, Canada

My definition of success involves the 3 F's - Family, Friends and Finances. Most would define success as having a large stately home, lots of money and fancy cars. Success in my world is having family who loves you, friends you can confide in and count on in tough times, and enough finances to do the things you want in life comfortably. In order to be successful you must set goals and targets which in turn create a path that you can follow to celebrate your achievements along the way.

My biggest success was starting a Mail Boxes Etc. franchise. Determination, hard work and being confident in my abilities helped me start up the store and build a client base that allowed our store to grow and continue to service the clients in an efficient manner. I chose the franchise model as it offered a clearly defined path in a business world that I had never ventured in to. By setting goals and targets within this model I was able to focus on networking with the other business owners within my city and build my business unique to my setting. We couldn't sit back and expect people to know what our business offered, we had to 'go out and get it'. This meant cold calling other businesses, offering incentives and educating them on what we were all about. Networking can build your business and in turn achieve goals and benchmarks that you set in your success model. Our clients became our friends and a support network and as our client base grew we were financially able to have a store that did not require support from our personal finances. To me, this was success within the first year - and we were proud of it!

—Kyla Foster, Entrepreneur

I feel successful because each step of my journey in life is a lesson on how to grow further. It's a darn good rhythm to be in.

—Kim Kapes, Author of "From Wags To Riches",
Dog Listener & Director of "In Harmony With Nature" Animal Haven,
www.inharmonywithnature.org, www.fromwagstorichesbook.com

Success in business or in personal life is an evolution; you are not born with it and must work hard to earn it. Perseverance and hard work = success.

To be successful at anything, one must have courage, taking risks, must be fully dedicated and exude quality leadership skills.

One must also adhere to the principle of: Are we gonna do it or are we just gonna talk about it?

—Ralph Askar, Chairman and CEO of Instant Imprints Franchising, Inc. www.instantimprints.ca

By making choices that are true to myself-doing what I feel is important and actively choosing which path I will take leaves me knowing that I've been able to create the environment that has allowed my children the space to become their own persons who can make wise decisions and look at life situations while being proud of their choices. This is how I see success in my life. Knowing that they see a "big picture" at their young ages leaves them with boundless opportunity for the future.

—Tamara Hockley, Self-employed single mom of three

To me, success is all about the quality of one's journey. It is not about reaching the end, but how one pursues the result with purpose and integrity, persisting through setbacks, and keeping one's "eye on the prize".

—Keith Taraba, Veterinarian and Entrepreneur

I am clear that one of the biggest secrets to success for me has been a willingness to say "YES".

Saying yes has pushed me outside of my "familiar zone" (the place where I know everything and feel in control -even if it is not always comfortable). And outside of my "familiar zone" is where life happens. It is the place where I get that butterfly sensation in my stomach or I can feel the sweat running down my arms and soaking my shirt. It is the place where I am present to each moment in front of me, truly experiencing my life as it unfolds, not stuck in reviewing my past or contemplating a future that seldom shows up exactly as I plan it.

In fact living my "YES" has taken me all over North America speaking and enriching lives. It has also brought the most incredible teachers and mentors to me as friends and co-workers and guiding lights.

—James Downie, Entrepreneur and Transformation Specialist,
www.JamesDownie.com

Success Defined for me has been creating a work style that was what I wanted. I work when I want to, with whom I want to and the hours I want to. I decide how much money I make and what kind of projects I take on. I push myself to take on projects that I have to do a lot of research on, and all of it is exciting because it includes the pursuit and thrill of helping other people.

—Verna Masuda, Entrepreneur

"Happiness=Success. Scientific research has demonstrated that happiness leads to better health, longevity (happy people live 9 years longer on average), coping strategies for dealing with stress, and performance. People who are happy with themselves, with their spouses or partners and family, and with their work are successful people. Research has also shown that friendship has a bigger effect on happiness than income. People who have enough money and lots of good friends are much happier than people who have lots of money but few friends. Setting goals and achieving them also plays a role in happiness. We find fulfillment in setting goals and then using our talents and abilities to attain them. The sense of fulfillment derived from successfully achieving our goals elevates our personal estimation of happiness. The best news of all is we can work at making ourselves happier in two ways: 1.) working on relationships and 2.) challenging ourselves by setting and then achieving goals. Happiness=Success!"

—Robbin Gibb, PhD, Assistant Professor,
Department of Neuroscience, University of Lethbridge

Success Defined for me is:

Success is a measure; a measure of how closely one comes to achieving their goal(s).

Therefore, in order to measure success or even discuss it, one must have a goal or goals.

Although the mnemonic below may seem a little cheesy, it does provide a structure on which to build thought as well as a simple reminder for me as to how successful I have been and continue to be. The acronym is **GOALS**.

1) Goals – I am often struck by the large number of people who stumble through life without any goals. I submit that if you have no goals, you will end up achieving nothing.

2) Opportunity – Sometimes the best opportunities are presented to us when we are given the occasion to help someone. Nothing is more satisfying than helping others.

But, the natures of the events are not nearly as important as it is to realize that all of us, regardless of our circumstances, will be given opportunity. Whether you believe in a Supreme Being or not, I guarantee you, you will be given the gift of opportunity.

The key is to recognize it. When opportunity knocks and it aligns with your goals, seize it. Every day, look for opportunity. If you remain on the lookout, you will find the opportunity to be successful in your life. Carpe diem!

3) Assess – Every once in a while one must sit back, relax and take stock.

Ask yourself questions like:

Did I accomplish what I set out to?

Do I have everything I want/need?

What part of my life do I need to improve upon?

What do I need to do to improve?

Every now and again I do examine where I'm at and where I would like to be as I move in to each stage of life. By assessing to what degree I have achieved my goals, I gain perspective and motivation.

It wouldn't be good to set goals, perhaps even write them down and prioritize and then forget about them. One must engage in continual assessment of one's goals.

4) Learning – There is always a lesson to be learned. No matter what happens, good or bad, negative or positive, there is always something to be learned. The trick is to search for it.

5) Success – I consider success to be a very personal thing. One cannot assess the success or lack thereof for another. It is something one can only do for one's self. It is directly connected to *your* goals.

I am successful because of the goals I set, my pursuit of them by seizing opportunity, by constant examination of where I'm at with my goals, because of my desire to learn and my own personal perspective.

I fully expect that my success will continue.

—Robert Cowie, B. Ed., M. Ed.

Success at the Vauxhall Academy of Baseball is not determined by wins/losses or how talented our team is -- it is rather a by-product of the individual development of each athlete and their growth as young men in these areas; athletically, academically, mentally, socially and baseball specific skill development.

The true definition of success of a youth sports program is interviewing and seeking feedback from former athletes who were NOT your best player(s). They will give you a true sense of whether your program is successful.

—Les McTavish, Head Coach & Director of Baseball Operations,
Vauxhall Academy of Baseball

Recently, while watching our grandson playing volleyball at an L.C.I. tournament, a young man named Danny Lyon told me he was writing a book. Danny asked if I would write something for his book - subject – what I think "Success" is?

I was a little surprised that Danny asked me, because, as far as the usual idea of success – meaning – "the gaining of wealth and position", I don't think I qualify. I have never wanted to be a wealthy person. Because Danny asked me, I decided that maybe he thought I had attained some kind of success.

The first goal I had was to determine in my own mind – What is Success?

I recalled that many, many years ago, while in grade twelve – the Year Book Editor was asking everyone the usual questions. One of which was – When you graduate, what is your ambition in life?

My answer to this was – "All I want to do with my life, is be successful at any one thing".

Now at 75 years, Danny has given me the task of trying to determine if I can define "success". Is success an accumulation of wealth and prestige? Maybe you can be a success by another definition?

I can say that I never made a lot of money!

My adult life started in a small town called Barons, Alberta

Barons was a great place to live but as most small towns, a good community life depends on a lot of people taking part in activities and volunteering to help keep the community active.

Our family, who had been in Barons since 1904, had always been active in the community. Therefore, as my generation came "of age" it was easy for me to become part of helping to keep things going.

For about 20 years, my wife Joyce and I tried to do our part. This ranged from being active in local sports participation, to coaching school sports, and belonging to different clubs as members as well as executives. This time included 9 years on our local school board.

It seems like we were involved heavily for fifteen years, or so, and looking back, I enjoyed every minute of our life in Barons.

In 1971, two friends from Calgary and I decided we would start a business in Lethbridge. The business would be the same type as they had in Calgary and be known as "Plainsman Sports". Unfortunately, they were both killed in a car accident before we even opened.

I decided to continue on with our plans, working with the two young widows as partners. This entailed leaving the farm and moving into Lethbridge.

A new life started for Joyce and I and our four sons.

Soon after our move to the city, I became involved again in coaching baseball teams, going on the board of the Chamber of Commerce, joining several clubs and eventually getting involved in politics.

For about 12 years we were very busy supporting our boys in their sports. They played baseball, hockey, football, and basketball. My wife estimated we spent about 4,000 hours at sports venues.

I coached baseball for many years in Lethbridge and had a great time. Over the years I coached many great young men and met many fine parents of these boys. We are still friends with many of these people.

As my coaching years were coming to an end, politics started interesting me. The first attempt was to try and get the nomination for a Federal Election.

I came in second – not so good! I next attempted to try at city council – this time I was about 100 votes from being elected.

A provincial election was coming up – so there I went again! I again came in second! My political life took a few years off – then I took up another attempt to get elected on city council – once again I just missed.

One could say that these "tries" were very discouraging – but as I look back, I don't feel that way at all. At least I tried and did the best I could.

I have saved the "Best for Last." Joyce and I celebrated our 52nd wedding anniversary last year. Our four sons have all turned out to be honest, ethical, level headed young men, who are raising our nine grandchildren to become people who can live in our society.

These four sons and our nine grandchildren are my success story!

So once again, what is Success?

1. Making lots of money – yes, to some people

2. Becoming a well known politician – yes, to some people

3. Becoming a winner in sports – yes, to some people

4. Becoming a winner in Life – yes

Many years ago, in the Lethbridge Civic Centre I saw a slogan – it said "When the Great Last Scorer Writes Against Your Name – He Does Not Ask – Did You Win or Lose – But How You Played The Game?"

There you go – I did my best!

I think I did reach my ambition!

I did become a success in one thing

I was a winner in Life

That is my definition of success

—**Ken Kotkas**

"What could I have in common with cream and dead fish? And what could that have to do with success?

At the age of one I was still in rubber pants. For those young ones that don't know what rubber pants are, they are what went on over the cloth diaper to keep the "ick!" in. At our family cottage my sister (age 4.5), cousin (age 6), mother and father were busy trying to get the speed boat out of the boat house and winch it down to the water. I was playing around and at some point it occurred to my mother that I wasn't in sight.

Curious by nature I had wandered off (and have many times since) so they formed a posse and had started to head for the woods. At the edge of the tree line my sister looked back and sighted my red pants bobbing in the water. My rubber pants filled with air (and God knows what else) and held my butt out of the water like a fisherman's red buoy. I was already floating past the head of the dock when my Dad dove in still wearing his hat, pipe, shoes and all.

They tell me I spit and sputtered a bit, like the old Johnson boat motor, but none the worse for wear; as God gives babies a survival instinct to hold their breath under water. I was changed, re-immersed into dry clothes including the life saving rubber pants and we did go back out for our boat ride.

Years later and long after I had forgotten my father's instinct to protect and my own built in mechanism to survive, I was back in the water determined to take my own life. And you can read about it in *From Suicide to Survival* (www.SuicidetoSurvival.com)

So what does this have to do with success?

My definition is when things get really tough, I mean *really* tough, take a minute, float to the top and then just keep hauling yourself out of the water."

—Cynthia Carpenter, Author and Health and Wellness Coach,
www.theinsidetrainer.com

There have been many successes throughout my life. Many tiny ones that culminated into something spectacular, to others more subtle and hidden behind the scenes. Successes from marrying my wife Molly and having four vibrant daughters, to buying millions of dollars worth of real estate and taking multiple inventions to the marketplace. Out of all of them, the one that most fervently comes to mind is the continuing success of being authentic (being ME) and owning my intuition and faith in my God-giving abilities to make a positive impact on others in this world.

—Keith Schmidt, Entrepreneur and Coach

Success is when a being starts thinking about what it wants, knows it will get there regardless of what hurdles it has to overcome and starts moving towards the realization of the idea.

—Paloma Baertschi-Herrera, Interspecies Communication Specialist and Life Energy Consultant for Animals LEB/T (www.SpeciesSpace.com)

My definition of success is to Love what I do for a living. Laugh freely. Love much and unconditionally. Appreciate the moment. Teach my children to do the same.

—Patti Knoles, Owner, Bakyta Design

On paper, my life is full of successes and I am extremely grateful. My dream as a kid was to play professional sport and I was blessed with enough talent to play both professional cricket and rugby on leaving school. I have wonderful friends, a loving family, have enjoyed promotions at work and more recently I have started my own business helping professional athletes secure new careers on retirement. I suddenly realized that success comes from the inside and cannot be truly judged by external displays of wealth or position. The only limitations are self-imposed and by making my dream a reality I am able to help even more people achieve their dreams along the way. Jones of Toledo couldn't have summed it up any better with the words "What I want for myself, I want for everybody." So, I strongly advise you to go out and grab it!

—Charlie Mulraine, Mentor and Career Coach, www.mulrainesport.com

I am a very young 65 year old man that has been married for 43 years. I have two children and 4 grandchildren.

One of my definitions for success is being happily married for all those years to a wonderful, loving and supportive wife. My children are great parents. They spend countless hours with their kids coaching sports, doing homework, hunting, wrestling, bike and motorcycle riding. They are always teaching and loving them. My wife says that I was a great teacher. That is my greatest success.

—Jim Adams, Businessman, Shreveport, Louisiana, www.adamspainting.net

Frank's thoughts on success…

How do we know if we have found success? Do we have any scars, any stories to tell about? Of course we do, we all do. I believe that success is in the journey because I believe the purpose of the journey in life is ultimately to learn, grow and progress. In another perspective I would say success is a lousy teacher. The challenge filled life experience garnered – this is the tutelage worth seeking. In a way we have it all backwards: that which we would typically consider as success is of little value, while the experiences that we often consider failure – these are the juicy bits worth savouring.

I like the way Earl Nightingale put it: "Success is the progressive realization of a worthy ideal"

So what worthy ideal are you "success-ing your way towards?" Why do we attempt to arrive without partaking of the journey? Why do we want the path of least resistance? Why do we think it will be better if we can avoid the process and somehow find a shortcut? Why do we want to resist the part that means the most?

When we attempt a life of only successful arrivals without any journeys we will look back and see we have missed what really matters most and success will be meaningless. When we work to eliminate the journey, we are working to create failure, rather than success. Therefore working to eliminate life's journey is the only true failure in life.

We need targets to shoot for, absolutely. The "points of arrival" are not what define our success – what we learn on the way *IS*. So get out those worthy ideas and enjoy the journey!

—**Frank Kickbush is an Author, Leadership Consultant, Trainer, Speaker and Training Developer. His latest book is:**
The Secrets of Self-Leadership – Map Your Destiny Using Your Inner Compass!
Visit www.frankkickbush.com for details.

"My success has spanned fifty years. It has taken me this long to discover true success in my life. As I relax by the fire and reminisce I have realized the significance of the past 50 years. I put my heart and soul into being a responsible parent and a good provider for my wife and kids. I know I was a parent that allowed my kids, a daughter and a son, to verbally and openly express their opinion and I know I responded in a respectful manner. As I review the past 22 years of being involved with raising a family I understand the importance in the development of a child's spirit.

I am proud as a parent. I cherish the time that I have spent with my kids and will continue to be proud of their accomplishments at whatever their future endeavours may be. Personally I cannot imagine a life without kids and I sincerely hope that they will educate their own kids about the importance of respecting people for who they are and respond to them accordingly. Life is a journey, enjoy the ride!

—Cam Hotel, Father of Two and Teacher, Brandon, Manitoba

Success is a journey toward progress in one's life and dreams. It is staying within the orbit of the two acronyms, SCORE and SMART. A more explicit definition of one's success is having to maintain a balance amongst several key elements of SCORE (Self- Discipline, Concentration, Optimism, Relaxation and Enjoyment) and, having a dream and realization of SMART goals (Specific, Manageable, Achievable, Realistic and Time bound).

—Van Visanatha, Entrepreneur & Owner of The UPS Store #36,
Calgary, Alberta

If you want to be successful you have to condition your mind for it. It all starts with your own definition of success followed by a strong desire of achievement and setting up a clear goal, whether if it is for getting a specific amount of money, improving your health, be promoted to a higher position, or any other achievement you want to accomplish in a specific period of time.

Again, it is a journey with ups and downs, but it is very important to keep the end in mind always feeling that you deserve it and you are capable of obtaining it.

—Misael Portillo, Founder & CEO, Gipsa, LLC

I define success first by *recognizing* my own chosen purpose for being here on earth. This **certainty** of my place in the world is like a magnet to all that I need as I live on this path that is my reason for being. As I am inducted into the knowledge of the mind and with the love that continually streams through me from the Universe, I embrace my own genuine success and choose to teach others to Live their own outstanding purpose.

—Marcie Downing, Singer/Songwriter/Recording Artist,
www.marciedowning.com

Real success is holding on to your vision long enough until others see it too, then leading them to victory. Seeing your dream being carried in the minds and hearts of men, woman and children alike and seeing them succeed, you know you have made a difference. It is the greatest reward the human heart can ever experience. It gives you a sense of Joy, Peace and Serenity that your life has purpose and that it so much more fulfilling when it is "not just about me".

—Gilbert Anderson

"I can say at this point in my life that success to me is overcoming the obstacles that I have dealt with and realizing that I can indeed become the person I want to be."

—Kim Fisher, Independent Representative, www.fhtmca.com/kimfisher

"Success is the deliberate continual motion of energy directed towards a worthy goal while fulfilling the infinites spirits highest potential within us."

—Paul Rink

"A successful person is one that discovers his/her Inner-Self, his/her own beauty, his/her own power, his/her own wisdom. This person goes on and goes further every day, because they finally found what they were looking for since the day they were born. Your life is successful, if you first of all found what really gives you chills, what makes you jump out of your bed in a very enthusiastic way in the morning and second, if you go for it!"

—Stefanie Vermeuken, Entrepreneur, www.stefanieVermeulen.com

To be truly successful is to be doing what you truly want.

It is to live and work in a harmonious environment in which you can continue to forever develop and learn from experience and people.

Choose the thing you really want and then make it true, going step by step.

I have done this several times in my life and one example is the Safer World Concept that I have originated.

Sweden, where I am from, is the first country and Safer Sweden is all over the country since February 2009.

When I am writing this, I am also preparing to launch in the US.

Improving the situation for those who have had a crime happen to them is something I really want to do.

I know from personal experience what was missing in 2005 when I was attacked. I know how much the concept we have created helps.

This is my success story. I wish you all the best with yours.

—Joakim Fohlman, Visionary Entrepreneur

Success is

- Knowing your purpose and staking your life on achieving it in spite of all opposition.

- Realizing that "failure" is not a step backwards but rather a step forward.

- Active creation of new habit patterns that achieve desired results.

- Having an open mind to other ideas and thoughts.

- Being able to accept no limitations.

- To be habitually persistent.

Like happiness, success cannot be bought. It is a choice of living, a state of mind.

An exciting journey which starts here and now once you realize that you are the creator of your own life. I love every minute of it.

—Jeffrey T. Skrob, Founder of the "Ultimate Space Challenge", Switzerland

To me, the definition of success is a four-step process:

1. Dreaming a really big, gargantuan dream;

2. Making a commitment to actually bring it into reality – this is a serious step;

3. Writing down whatever action steps you can think to take;

4. Actually TAKING those steps, trusting that the way will continue to unfold for you.

One of my favourite personal success stories has to do with where I live – a penthouse on a big rock over the ocean with 300-degree views.

Initially, I had moved to a lower condo unit in this rare Laguna Beach complex, which was magic enough. But it was only a matter of time before I discovered the penthouse unit up above. I knew it had to be mine – only issue: long-term renters were already living there.

The process began in November.

First step – I used one of Bob Proctor's Goal Cards to write my "result" of having moved to the penthouse. As he taught me, I wrote the goal in past-tense terms, as if it had already been achieved. I carried the card with me everywhere and daily wrote the affirmation several times in my journal.

Then, I went to the Board of the condo association to find the name and location of the condo owner. She lived in Colorado. I called her and, after introductions, told her that I'd like to move to her penthouse unit, as I didn't believe her renters would be living there much longer. I suggested that I send her a security deposit check to ensure that I'd be the one she called when they gave her intent to vacate.

She was warm and friendly but assured me the renters were going nowhere. They were long-termers who had been paying for years and they had yet another 2 years on their contract.

Again, I told her that I thought their situation was changing and that I'd be happy to send her the security deposit. She laughingly agreed and told me she'd hold it in her files.

As soon as I got off the phone with her, I called my existing landlord and told her that I'd likely be moving in the next few months to the penthouse and that I'd give her as much notice as possible. She thought this was fine as she was actually thinking of spending her time at the beach that following summer – if I vacated, she'd simply take over her own condo.

From there, I rented a storage unit for six months – through May of the following year. The penthouse offered a great deal more space – I obviously needed more furniture. So, I began choosing the colors of my walls, determining my décor and buying the furniture, art, lighting and outdoor deck décor and stuffing it away in the storage unit. My friends thought I was absolutely nuts – but this didn't deter me. I was holding a vision of living in the penthouse and I was acting in whatever way I could to "act as if" I was already there.

I changed my routine into the complex, too. When I'd come home with groceries, I'd carry them with me up the stairs to the penthouse before working my way back down to my existing condo. I'd stand on the public walkway just outside the penthouse and watch the sun come up. I'd run on the beach and look up at the penthouse with a big, wide smile in my face. "My place. So happy and grateful I'm living there."

I'm sure you can already guess the ending to the story. On May 21st, she called me out of the blue to tell me that "of all the crazy things" her renters had just notified her to vacate. They had decided - on the spur of the moment - to purchase a home in a neighbouring town. Their closing date was fast approaching – when would I be available to move? I assured her I could be in as soon as the following week. We agreed to terms and she mailed me the contract.

- My storage unit's contract expired on May 31st, of course.
- My existing landlord had already made "hopeful plans" to move into her condo on June 5th, and was delighted I called.
- I began painting my penthouse walls (with paint I'd already purchased and stored) on May 28th.
- Two days later, my movers hauled in all my new furniture.

Success never comes by accident. It's a dream. A commitment. An action plan. And action in the best way you know how, no matter how small those steps might seem to be.

What's YOUR dream?

—Diane Armitage, Armitage, Inc., Marketing Writer, Website Fixer, Ongoing Internet Strategy & Campaign, www.FixYourLameWebsite.com

AFTERWORD

A Marathon is 42.2 kilometres or 26.2 miles.

$$\begin{array}{r} 100 \\ -\ 31 \\ \hline 69 \end{array}$$

We were sitting around watching TV one evening when my then 10 year old daughter, Maggie, asked a question she already knew the answer to, "Your goal is to complete 100 marathons, right?" "How many have you done?" she asked. I had completed 31. Maggie took out a blank piece of paper and wrote in very big numbers (perhaps to make sure the old man could see them), speaking out loud as she wrote "one-hundred minus thirty-one equals…sixty-nine?!? Wow, you don't have that many done!" I asked her what she was getting at. She boldly stated, "I think a good goal for you is to have 50 marathons completed by your 50th birthday."

And then there was silence. I am sure smoke was coming out of my ears as I thought hard about what she was challenging me to do and if I was up for the challenge. Another example of one's network making a person look outside of their comfort zone.

There were only 22 months left until my 50th birthday and 19 marathons to complete if I was crazy enough to try. I explained to Maggie that I would have to do close to a marathon a month to reach the goal. She sarcastically replied, "So?"

After much debate about training, recovery and travel around that many marathons in that short of a time frame – all of which she didn't really care about - I asked her to set up a schedule for me and I would consider it.

Maggie's first schedule included marathons in Australia, China, Africa and Europe. Although, many were on my goals list, they weren't do-able in the short time window. I wanted to build vacations around those – not pop in, run, and pop out. We agreed to rework the schedule together and therefore, by default, I accepted Maggie's challenge.

In May, 2006, 21 months until my 50th, the trek for **50 by 50** started with Vancouver, Red Deer and Lethbridge marathons in that very first month. The schedule Maggie set up had me completing marathon #50 in August, 2007 – 16 months after starting. I was right on schedule until June 2007. While attempting the 3rd of 3 marathons in back-to-back-to-back weekends, I pooped out in Helena, Montana, and completed the half-marathon instead.

After the Calgary, Missoula and San Francisco marathons in July, finishing Edmonton in August, 2007 was #49, instead of the planned #50.

Word got around that I needed one more marathon to reach the goal Maggie had set. Ideas on where to run and how to make it special came from many supporters. It was then that I received another phone call from Maggie.

She said, "I think your 50th marathon should be my 1st."

Now that was a way to make it special. She was now 11 years old and apparently willing to move way out of her comfort zone to help her old man. A year-round soccer player, I was confident in her abilities and asked her to pick the marathon.

"I'll phone you right back," she said and hung up before I could say goodbye.

This started a series of rapid, brief calls from her, and always with the "I'll phone you right back" ending.

"I want to run the New York City Marathon". I explained that it would be full.

Next call, "Tell me about this Washington, DC place. What is there?" It was full too.

And so it continued. I finally suggested she check the date of the Long Beach, California Marathon, one of my goal marathons. We were going to be on the Bob Proctor Cruise to the Mexican Riviera in October and I thought, perhaps, the date of the Long Beach Marathon might line-up with that trip.

Another call, "Tell me what's in Long Beach. Will there be shopping?" I suggested that we would be coming off a 7-day cruise. Shopping probably wouldn't be a priority. I asked, "Does the date line-up?" She replied with a "Yes". "Is this the *one*?" She said, "Yes".

When I got back to my laptop I confirmed the dates were correct, made the changes to our travel arrangements and entered the Long Beach Marathon.

Problem #1: The age restriction was 13 years old and on race day. Maggie would only be several weeks short of her 12th birthday.

I called her and asked, "Are you comfortable about lying about your age in order to get into the race?" I got a lecture on lying (who was the parent here?) followed by questions on organizers asking for identification.

"I'll phone you right back," she said.

This time the delay between phone calls was quite long. Maggie was not comfortable with this lying thing at all. She called back and agreed only because of the importance of my 50th marathon. As far as I was concerned, it being her *1st Marathon* was way, way more important.

The Bob Proctor Cruise was ultra-fantastic. We docked in San Diego, drove to Long Beach, checked in, and headed down to the Marathon Fitness Expo to check out the offerings and pick up our race packages. Maggie's ID concerns were not a concern.

Up bright and early the next morning, Connie drove us to the starting area, saw us start the race and then went back to rouse the boys out of bed.

My 50th marathon ended up being very special indeed. Maggie was a joy to run with. Lots of questions and conversation.

A couple of miles into the race the course doubled back to the start area. There was a tent set up where volunteers were serving up a pancake breakfast. Maggie could smell them. "Will we be able to eat pancakes when we finish the race," she asked. I promised her that we would go anywhere she wanted for pancakes after the race. About a mile later, Maggie told me that the only thing keeping her going was the thought of pancakes when she finished. I told her to hold that thought front and centre (as there was a long, long way to go yet).

People along the way provided Maggie with words of encouragement. Around mile 12 we were passed by two ladies who congratulated Maggie and asked her how old she was. Hesitating a second or two, Maggie uncomfortably blurted out, "13". The ladies were amazed, congratulated Maggie again and then started to put some distance between us. I told Maggie that because she had her race number on her chest, her timing chip on her shoe and was almost half-way through the race, it was okay to tell people how old she really was. With a great look of relief she said, "Serious?" and then sprinted off to catch the ladies. I heard Maggie say, "I am sorry. I lied about my age". Both ladies immediately responded that they knew she had to be older. Then Maggie said, "No, not older. I am only 11 and didn't want to say my real age because you are supposed to be 13 to enter." Silence followed for several strides with both ladies staring at her. They then raved and congratulated her again, this time with an exclamation mark. Maggie responded with a thank-you and – the most important part to her – apologized once again for lying.

I like to tease Maggie that she ate her way through the marathon. I pretty much stick to water during a race and rarely eat anything offered at aid stations or by people who line the race route – oranges, bananas, Power Bar chunks, pretzels, peanuts, jujubes, etc. Apparently famished, Maggie never missed anything. At mile 20, a lady was just getting a small table set up to offer pretzels, nuts, and sweets to runners. Maggie saw the goodies, which were in a clear plastic bag, and announced her disappointment to me that the lady was not set up yet (how dare she). The lady heard and invited Maggie to feast on the offering while continuing to set up. I thought Maggie would be a bit embarrassed that the lady had heard her comment and would just thank the lady and continue on. Nope. She wheeled around, went back, opened the bag and visited while munching on pretzels. I had to stop and wait.

Just after mile marker 21, a male runner ahead of us stopped running and abruptly sat down in the middle of the road. His buddies running with him tried to get him remobilized but he refused. He wasn't injured – he had just had enough. His day was over and he became quite abusive when his friends wouldn't just leave him there. I told Maggie that this fellow was why, no matter how slow I had gotten over the years, I never finished last – because, in every race, there were always people that quit. This led to a long discussion of why people quit and my belief that the only way to fail in anything is to quit.

> *"Once you learn to quit, it becomes a habit."*
>
> —Vincent Lombardi

There were several times during the race that Maggie brought up quitting. I asked her how she would feel telling people that she had made it almost to the end and then, when she needed to dig the deepest, she quit (like the fellow sitting on the road). I also told her that, "Once you cross the finish line, no one can ever take it away, whether you run another marathon or not." Maggie then listed several reasons as to why she could not and would not quit – sore but not that tired, no injury forcing her to stop, embarrassment of telling friends that she quit, and bragging rights if she finished. At 11 years old, on the verge of successfully completing her first marathon, she created her personal "Desperation Factor" on why she couldn't quit.

And she didn't quit. We crossed the finish line with our arms held high and both of our goals in the "success" column. **And a father extremely proud of his daughter.**

Riding high on Maggie's inspiration and success, I completed the Phoenix Marathon in January, about two weeks before my 50th birthday. Overall, she had inspired me to complete 20 marathons in 21 months and a total of 51 by 50.

One never knows where inspiration will come from or from whom. If a 10 year old girl can inspire someone to stretch and give 19 marathons in 21 months a try, what might someone in *your* network inspire you to stretch towards? Maggie's inspiration, challenge and holding me accountable caused me to overachieve – by choice. This is what I believe utilization of your network causes – growth, success and achieving things you thought were impossible (or just a dream).

The key was that I had "exposed" what my marathon goals were to my network. And it was my network support – in this case Maggie Lyon – who got me off my behind and out the door taking the action towards attainment.

 DANNY DIAMOND SUCCESS TIP:

She got me to "do" the "doing". This is what your network can do for you.

My recommendations for added inspiration to take action and to keep you moving forward to exponential success are:

"Must Have" Books:

1. "Me to We" by Craig and Marc Kielburger (www.freethechildren.com)

2. "Unstoppable" by Cynthia Kersey

3. "You Were Born Rich" by Bob Proctor

4. "Secrets of the Millionaire Mind" by T. Harv Eker

5. "Millionaire Mindset" by Gerry Robert

6. "177 Mental Toughness Secrets of the World Class", by Steve Siebold (www.mentaltoughnesssecrets.com)

7. "The E-Myth Revisited" by Michel Gerber (www.e-myth.com)

8. "Outliers" by Malcolm Gladwell

Ultra-Fantastic Programs:

1. Unstoppable Challenge (www.unstoppable.net)

2. Peak Potentials Training (www.peakpotentials.com)

3. Bob Proctor Network (www.bobproctor.com)

4. Bill Gove Speech Workshop (www.speechworkshop.com)

5. The Mastery of Self-Expression (www.themasteryworkshops.com)

6. Millionaire Mindset Course (www.gerryrobert.com)

7. And for those that desire to "Create the life you REALLY want", please visit www.procoachsystem.com and get to know Master Coach Andrew Barber-Starkey.

The choice is yours. It always has been. I encourage you to explore and utilize all of the possibilities and phenomenal opportunities that lie within your great network.

My desire is that you will better utilize and expose yourself to your network, share and analyze your successes; and forever stretch outside your comfort zone and the same old thing. And by doing so, become a "High-Flyer", in all aspects of life.

"Expose Yourself For Success"